About the author

Yvonne Joye was raised in Cork City and graduated from University College Cork in 1990 with a Bachelor of Arts in German and Sociology.

The following year she moved to Dublin where she worked in the financial sector services sector for almost a decade. Since 2005 she has worked on a part-time basis in event management. She lives in Dublin with her husband and three children.

TEN FINGERS
&
TEN TOES

Yvonne Joye

BOOK REPUBLIC

A BOUTIQUE PUBLISHING PRESS

PUBLISHED IN 2010 BY BOOK REPUBLIC

Book Republic, Office 19, Dunboyne Business Park,
Dunboyne, Co. Meath, Ireland.

http://www.bookrepublic.ie
info@bookrepublic.ie

ISBN: 978-1-907221-04-0

5 4 3 2 1

The paper used in this book comes from wood pulp of
managed forests. For every tree felled, at least one tree is
planted, thereby renewing natural resources.

A CIP catalogue record for this book is available from the
British Library.

DEDICATION

For my four children: Adam, Luke, Laura, and Matthew.

ACKNOWLEDGEMENTS

I owe a great debt of gratitude to my parents, Patrick and Cora Reidy, my greatest yardstick, for consistently putting to one side their own feelings, and letting me run riot with mine. A big thank you also to my family, whose ability to laugh through life has made me who I am.

I wish to acknowledge the help and support of my dearest friends (you know who you are) who I have called upon far too often over the years, yet who have never wavered in their loyalty and love.

A badge of honour must go to my kids for letting me disappear every evening for months while I wrote this book.

I also wish to pay a special tribute to the staff at Holles Street Hospital and Crumlin Children's Hospital; their ordinary working days are full of extraordinary events.

Finally, I want to thank my husband Niall for surrendering his privacy and for his constant support and encouragement. Without him, I could not have written this or, for that matter, function, smile or be.

Contents

I

The Bad News Room

"Let me get this straight, you're telling me that if one of your babies had a hole in its heart that would just be dandy?" *For feck's sake!* "So, as far as you're concerned, this is all grand? This isn't the end of the world for any of us?" *How very easy for you!* "I don't think you get it," I said, trying but failing to cling to civility in my tone. "I really don't think you get it!"

I was sitting on the edge of a seat in a small neat room in the National Maternity Hospital in Holles Street, Dublin city. Both my legs kept jigging up and down, up and down. I was huddled over a hospital phone, and while the fingers of my left hand played with the twirls in the cord, my right hand held the handset tightly against the side of my head; so tight that little spots of condensation were appearing on the black surface. It was as if the closer I held it, the less room there would be for confusion between us. That, apparently, wasn't working.

"Are you hearing me, Frances?" I asked again, and then slowly I repeated, "They think my baby has a hole in its heart." *There! Now will you stop being so bloody calm and shagging reasonable about the whole thing? What is wrong with her? What in God's name is wrong with her?*

There wasn't a hint of panic in her voice. Not even a token broken voice. A few tears might have been nice. I mean, it wasn't as if I was asking her to lose the plot altogether; though had she done so, I think I would have really appreciated it. *What is wrong with her?*

Okay, so she was a paediatrician. She could have, might have, possibly seen and heard a whole lot worse. But this was me! Me! Her fellow struggling, self-berating mother, her partner-in-crime with the vino, her girlfriend, her sister-in-law for God's sake! I wasn't a patient. I wasn't one of her cases. *So stop with the doctor stuff already. Freak out with me here a little, why don't you?* God knows, I was totally freaked out. I couldn't believe it; I really couldn't believe it. *This is not happening; this cannot be happening! This is not real; someone tell me this is not real.*

The room in which I sat belied the drama unfolding in it. It was just so ordinary. The walls reminded me of the walls we had in school, bumpy and wet with condensation; the kind of walls that if you wanted to wallpaper them, you'd probably need to plaster them first. *Jesus Christ, plasterwork? My world is falling apart and I'm worried about the add-on effort of plastering hospital walls. Next I'll be analysing the colour!*

Yellow. Fried egg yellow. *Who in God's name picked that?* Easy know they didn't have to live with it. Only passers-by like me. Momentarily suspended. Trapped.

There was a crucifix on the wall along with a loud clock. *When did I last hear the ticking of a clock?* Once again, I was reminded of school. God, that whole place was making me feel I was back there, sitting in the principal's office, staring at the crucifix, hearing the rhythm of a heavy wall clock, knowing I was in a mass amount of trouble, and waiting for all Hell to break lose. The only difference now was I was in a hospital, and Hell was already upon me.

There was a chair in the room, more of a loveseat than a chair (I supposed that was for if a couple were there), a table, and a telephone. Next to the telephone was a box of tissues. This was definitely a "bad news" room. *A bad news room!* I supposed all hospitals had to have rooms like this—a "delicate situation" room, a "knowing nothing else to do with these people" room. I had just never figured that the National Maternity Hospital would need one. I mean, Holles Street was a maternity hospital, a happy place, good things happened there. It was a place where life was delivered and people arrived with balloons and flowers. It was a fun place where baby faces were matched with adult ones, where some thought they had delivered the most beautiful baby in the world, whilst others hoped theirs would get better-looking.

I had always thought that's what maternity hospitals were all about. Always. God knows what I ever thought happened to all the sad cases. *All the sad cases.* I had never considered that. Alternative versions of the Holles Street experience had never entered my consciousness, my world. *Well, that's all changed now.*

I had just been told that the baby I was carrying, my fourth child, had a problem with its heart. I didn't know how serious it was, and I wasn't going to know until the baby was born. I heard the doctor mention a hole in the heart but, after that, I really didn't hear much else.

I was on my own, it was Thursday, 17 December 2002, and I was due to deliver on 14 February 2003. I was 34 years old.

My obstetrician told me there was some malformation in the baby's heart that would have to be righted upon birth. For this to happen, the baby would need to be transported immediately after birth to Crumlin Children's Hospital on the other side of the city, and undergo emergency surgery. *Planned emergency surgery, I suppose.*

Okay, so maybe this wasn't the end of the world. Maybe this wasn't the most serious condition to befall a human being, and maybe it wasn't the worst thing ever to happen to anyone. But it was definitely the worst thing to ever happen to me and, without doubt, the worst thing to happen to one of my children.

When I next spoke my voice was softer: "Really, Frances, do you think it will be okay? Really? I suppose it has all been done before, hasn't it? It's just a hiccup, isn't it? A big hiccup, but just a hiccup all the same, yeah?" *Last question*: "How am I going to tell Niall?" *My husband; oh poor Niall!*

Poor Niall? Poor Niall! At this point in time, "poor" Niall has only one shagging worry in the world—guilt at not making it to the scan. He had gotten caught in traffic around Drogheda and was feeling crap about not making it down in time. He felt crap. Jesus, I envied him. How I would love for that to be the only thing to make me feel crap today.

My energy deserted me, and I began to crumble. I was still sitting in the loveseat. The leg jigging had stopped, but now my whole body was rocking to and fro. I emitted a sequence of little snorts, to which Frances had no idea how to respond. This was perhaps a good thing because when she had tried to say the right thing before, I just annihilated her. She got the brunt of it—my total disbelief and horror. She was my first port of call. Niall should have gotten all that, but as I couldn't get through to him, she was up next.

It was probably better that I spoke to her first. Apart from her professional credentials, and my ties to her family-wise (she is my brother Dermot's wife), she had been particularly good to me over the past year, not merely as a sister-in-law, but as a real friend. She has a wonderful knack of calmness about her, with an in-built capacity to put everything in perspective and not get caught up in the drama of things. If there was ever a time I needed some of that, it was then and there. I needed her to soothe me, to take away the sting, to give it all meaning and put it in context, yet when she had tried to do just that, I lambasted her.

Still, it really was better that I didn't get through to Niall straight off. I was far too consumed with my own shock to have delivered the news to him in any coherent manner. He deserved better than that. *Haven't I received a very measured and clear delivery of the news? If only I could remember all of it!* He merited the very same. *So, how am I going to tell him? How in God's name am I going to put it to him?*

I did a little role-play: "Hi Niall, yeah, yeah I had the scan… a little bit of bad news though… that small worry we had… yeah… a little bit of a bigger problem… mmm… the baby… it's the heart… there's something wrong with it." I wouldn't mention the "hole in the heart" thing. I couldn't do that to him, not on the phone anyway. You tended not to hear anything else after that was said.

None of this fit with me; it really didn't—none of it at all. I am no "mother earth" but I really hated to think that my baby's first moments of life would be all about him being taken away from me, bundled into an ambulance, and driven halfway across the city. I understood that it was all for the good of my baby and, of course, I had heard of this happening to other people, but, may God forgive me, to my mind those people were always people with a "history", and because of their "history" I assumed their expectations were different. I, on the other hand, was normal—no great shakes but, Hell, when it came to having babies, I generally followed the rules; my only aberration was going 18 days over on my first pregnancy.

I reminded myself of a spiel we were given in one of the antenatal classes I attended when expecting my first child. The class leader was a mid-wife, and I think she must have been addressing any romantic notions we had about childbirth. I remember her telling us of one woman who had wanted to have a natural birth and breastfeed her child. Due to complications, she ended up having an emergency caesarean section, and to compound matters further, the breastfeeding wasn't working out for her. The mid-wife explained that this woman, nonsensically, felt like a failure. The mid-wife was emphatic in her conclusion—no failure here ladies, that woman had a healthy baby. Moral of the story: the pregnancy is not all about you; it's all about having a healthy baby.

I told myself to grow up. I consoled myself with the fact that I had been very grown up about Niall not making it to the scan. In truth, I hadn't been put out by that at all. *Easy be grown up.* In fairness, things had conspired against him. It wasn't his fault. He had sounded so very frustrated when he phoned to let me know, and he was falling over himself with apologies. 1011, 007 / 155·937092

"It'll be grand," I told him. "Just grand. Relax, I am fine."

Fine. And indeed I had been fine sitting on my own in that waiting room, just over an hour ago. *Was that only an hour ago?* Waiting for a scan that was to change everything. I had been more concerned with the comings and goings of those around me, enjoying the fact that I could observe everything without the distraction of a conversation. It was wonderful not to have to talk to anyone. A relief not to have to think of something to say which, unfortunately, seems to be a lifetime habit with me.

I suppose, generally, I talk too much. I know I could do with talking less. Yet, for whatever reason, I somehow always feel the need to fill a silence, cover a gap, pass a comment, or colour in an already painted scene. There is a lovely song that goes, "You say it best when you say nothing at all;" well that would never be me. Never. However, sitting in that waiting room, waiting on my scan, surrounded by strangers, with no children making demands, no husbandly enquiries, and no friends calling to make arrangements, I was, to all intents and purposes, most content. I took in all those around me, and if I had had someone to talk to, I would most likely have commented that you could tell that everyone else there were first-time parents because all the men were present.

As I waited, I thought that Niall had been ambitious in the first place to think he could have made it. He had a mad schedule at the moment and, at any rate, his presence really wasn't all that necessary. What I was doing in Holles Street on that day in December was routine. It was an indulgence of a kind doctor to quell a small concern of a loyal patient. I wasn't even really concerned. This was going to be a good news scan, a scan that was going to put to rest a teeny weeny concern I had over my baby's heartbeat. The good doctor was affording me this scan to give me peace of mind for Christmas.

Peace of mind!

"I'll call you on my way home," I had told Niall. "Carmel [a very good friend of mine] is feeding the kids. Do you want me to grab something for us to eat?" How lovely to have had things like that on my mind.

As time passed, the room began to empty. Tiredness was overwhelming me. My interest in the comings and goings was beginning to wane, and I had had enough of my own company. I looked at my watch. I had been waiting for over an hour. I was starting to regret having pushed for the appointment.

It was in the middle of those mad days in the run up to Christmas, and I had so much to do. We had spent the previous six months extending our house and had only just returned four days ago, after a turbulent few months of living outside our home. Now all I wanted was for home to feel like home again, and what I wanted more than anything else was for everything to get back to normal.

The waiting continued, and I was getting impatient. I really needn't have pushed this. I should have listened to the doctor when he said the scan wasn't necessary. *Why didn't I just leave well enough alone?* Because I was worried. Despite all the assurances, I was worried. I knew the baby's heartbeat was not right. After three healthy babies, I had gotten a sense of how things are supposed to be. This time round, I felt something was missing. It had come to light in September, the first time I heard it.

There truly isn't anything quite like that lovely, fast moving, train-like noise of a baby's heartbeat, the only giveaway of a baby in the early stages of its development. It is the best sound in the world and, upon hearing it, I always felt a great sense of relief take over as I surrendered to the excitement of what was happening to my body.

This time, that wasn't happening. That day in September, the heartbeat had sounded strange, odd. It sounded like there was a double beat or, perhaps, that the doctor was missing the heartbeat altogether and was just picking up my digestive system and the odd noises that go on in people's tummies. Whatever it was, it wasn't right. I'm a bit of an optimist, a "glass half full" kind of person, and as my doctor continued his examination that September day, I remember looking at his face, waiting for him to break a smile or ask me to bear with him because he hadn't quite gotten it yet.

He didn't do that. Neither, I must say, did he look worried or concerned. He stood up, pulled my shirt back over my tummy, and gave some wonderful explanation as to why my baby's heartbeat sounded like it did, and how it would right itself, if not by my next visit in October, then later in the pregnancy. *Phew! Great. Terrific. Nothing wrong. Brilliant explanation even.* I didn't understand it, but no matter. As far as I was concerned, everything was spot on. Hunky dory.

Driving home though, I got a little niggly feeling, and I just couldn't get rid of it. Funny, Niall wasn't with me that day either. Now, just for the record, I am not on a solo run here. I suppose that time round, I was altogether more grown up (that expression again). It was my fourth pregnancy, and I was a veteran of sorts. Previous pregnancies had all gone like clockwork. I never had any funny discharges, I never had any spots of bleeding, and I never knew any pregnancy traumas (or any other traumas for that matter). I always believed that in that area of my life, I would be normal, just plain old normal. It's an exceptional thing to be normal in pregnancy, however.

Of course, when I first started out in baby bearing, I wasn't so nonchalant. In fact, in previous pregnancies our doctor's appointments were cornerstones in our lives, and to have a scan was a near spiritual affair—a "meaning of life" moment or a "moment in time" experience.

All these things still held true for us, but by the time we were going for our fourth child, Niall had taken on a big new job, and we were already planning the mammoth task of a house extension. Our focus lay with organising our living arrangements outside the family home, at the cheapest price possible, and with minimum disruption to the kids' lives. As if that could ever happen!

The bills kept mounting. I wasn't working and hadn't been for the past five years. I was a stay-at-home Mum, despite our financial situation. Things were tight, very tight, so the last thing I was going to be in the midst of it all was a pregnant diva. Going to the doctor on my own was no big deal; Niall proving himself in his job and guaranteeing us all an income was.

When I came home from that September scan (home was a shell at that stage, with building work having commenced in July), I found Niall talking to the foreman. My husband is a very good looking guy (this is my prerogative, so run with it—I did marry the guy after all), and though my girlfriends would often ask me whether there were any "Diet Coke ad" guys working on site, none of the builders could hold a candle to him. Not that I didn't fully check out the prospect first! That day in early September, however, standing in the upheaval of our home in his impeccable dark navy suit and crisp white shirt, with his skin still dark from the summer, I thought he really looked too young to be so grown up and in charge. As he saw me approach, he walked towards me and led me away from the commotion he had been overseeing. He helped me duck under a ladder [*bad luck*] and step over a beam into the relative normality of the kitchen, the last vestige of our home.

He was about to launch into the latest unfolding drama in our never-ending building saga, when I spoke over him. I just blurted out that the baby's heartbeat was funny. I spoke without any feminine hysterics or prophecies of doom. It was a statement of fact. I promptly followed this with the doctor's assurances that all was well and told him that the doctor himself had appeared unconcerned.

Niall just looked at me. He was leaning against the sink, and I was thinking to myself, "I wish he'd move, his suit will be ruined."

He still said nothing. I could hear war breaking out in another part of the house. *I really wish the bloody builders would keep their shagging language down!* Niall remained still and quiet, just looking at me. He's a bit like that though, even under normal circumstances—he has that silent thing going on! He didn't automatically accept the doctor's assurances. I think he had a niggly feeling himself. He didn't throw himself at me or try to make light of things. No, he just stood there by the sink [*please move*] like he was trying to figure out something in his head. He definitely had a niggly feeling. Finally, in the building site that was our home, with our three kids playing precariously around us, builders effing and blinding at each other, and the consistent banging of doors at the mercy of constant draughts, he simply shrugged and said, "I suppose we just have to trust the guy. He is the foetal expert for God's sake!"

I don't think either of us quite bought it though. Nor did we buy it in October and November when my subsequent visits told the same story. Seeing my disappointment and growing unease, my obstetrician conceded that we should have a scan, but he presented this to me in a way that suggested it was merely to put all my concerns to rest—nothing to worry about. That was what had led me to that waiting room— that scan—and the subsequent bad news room on that dark December day, five days before Christmas.

This was, in fact, my second scan. My first real scan had been at close to 20 weeks, when the baby was the size of a nail on an adult's baby finger—that never ceases to amaze me. Apparently, this size isn't conducive to the detection of heart abnormalities, or so I was later told.

And so, I proceeded into the examination room for the scan. The examination room was really a high bed or stretcher, surrounded by curtains on three sides. There were a series of these examination rooms in what is, in essence, one big communal scanning department. The sounds in this room gave me the feeling that I had stepped onto the set of *20,000 Leagues Under the Sea*.

I settled myself up on the bed. At the best of times, I find this a bit of an achievement, though infinitely more applaudable when heavily pregnant. Amazing they haven't developed something a bit more conducive, though this was a few years ago, so maybe that has changed now.

Of course, ever the girl, the other distraction I had was how I was looking. You think you look well leaving the house after carefully choosing clothes to ensure minimum fuss for this very procedure but, somehow, as I was arranging myself so that the doctor could rub the gel on my tummy, I felt terribly self-conscious. I decided I had gotten the clothes all wrong. Again.

I failed to push my trousers down far enough [*he might think I am coming on to him*] so, invariably, the doctor had to amend my arrangement, which he did subtly. He said he wanted to protect my clothes from the gel, but really it was an effort to get full access to my bump. *I must remember for future reference that my pubic hairline is almost on show. I won't have him need to do this again.*

He started moving the sonogram over me—up, down, and across. Little dotted white lines were showing up on the screen. His focus was the middle of a floating black blob. I could see the spine. *My baby!* The doctor didn't speak, and a second doctor came into the room. He did the same thing. The movement over my tummy was starting to irritate me. The constant rolling back and forth, up and down, side to side—I got restless. A throb had developed in the side of my head, and I felt myself beginning to perspire. I wanted to shift my body, but I remained still. By nature, I felt compelled to speak, but I tried to stop myself. No conversation, no questions, no news. *Good.*

I could hear the banter of the nurses outside the curtain and their giggles over some in-house joke. *God, I want to be them. I wish I wasn't here. I really, really wish I wasn't here. Please God, don't let anything be wrong with the baby; please God, don't let anything be wrong.*

It must have been over half an hour before they stopped the rolling of the sonogram. The second doctor left and my own doctor began wiping the gel from my belly. He then handed me some clean towels so I could finish the job myself—nothing unusual. He allowed me to gather myself together. I got back to a more dignified posture, and he helped me off the bed. Everything seemed normal—except for the silence and the expression on my doctor's face.

My legs were weak as he asked me to follow him. We entered the "bad news" room, though I didn't know it to be such at the time. He invited me to sit down in the loveseat while he sat on the table, pushing the box of tissues to one side.

In the bad news room, he told me some bad news.

2

The Throwaway Comment

The events of that December day had their roots in another December day a year previous, Christmas 2001—a time that marked the starting point of so many things to come. Christmas—the best time of the year. People say Christmas is more about the anticipation than the actual event. Me, I take Christmas in two parts. The build up: 6 weeks, 8 weeks, three months…, and the celebration: 7 days. I love both parts equally.

Part one is the shopping, the lights, the carols, the madness. Christmas starting right after Halloween suits me just fine. From long lunches, to silly parties, to endless discussions on outfit choices, Christmas brings out the teenager in me, only better because we spend money as if we have it, plus I have a guaranteed score! Part one of Christmas as a parent is the next best thing to experiencing Christmas as a child. The innocent faces, the tangible excitement, the repetitive vows to be good, the endless Santa questions, the false explanations, the gammy logistics, and the prayers for snow.

By Christmas Eve we're at fever pitch. Niall usually has the laptop out since 11 a.m., and three small faces are always pressed up against the screen, plotting Santa's route from the North Pole. First stop: Australia. Of course this only ensures bedlam later when the bright children we have reared calculate Santa's speed, and by the time he reaches Western Europe, the kids have gauged his approximate time of arrival in South County Dublin. They are most plausible in their arguments when his estimated time of arrival is 1.30 a.m. and decide that subsequent access to the Christmas tree ought to be granted no later than 2 a.m.

In our earlier years of parenting, I was appointed as Santa's "special helper". This was a tradition born out of a time when the kids were too young to appreciate Santa or Christmas. Niall and I, only bursting for our second chance at Christmas, and too impatient to wait a year or two when the children would be old enough to appreciate the festivities, decided to introduce a bit of excitement of our own. Granted, our excitement was more adult in nature and involved me dressing up in a somewhat alluring "Santa's helper outfit" and working my magic! By Christmas 2001, however, that particular type of magic was waning. We couldn't get the kids to sleep.

"Can I have another glass of water, pleeease?" one of our children would invariably ask.

"No, you'll be up all night!"

"I'm too hot!"

"Kick the duvet off!"

"Is he here yet?"

"No, and at this rate, I doubt he'll be coming at all!"

"I'm scared; make sure you tell Santa we want the presents under the tree, not up here."

"He would never do that!"

"Can we get up, now?"

"Nooooooo!" we both would shout.

With our changing circumstances, and our growing family, my role of "helper" was downgraded to that of "lookout", for which no defined costume was required. Being lookout wasn't my thing, however, and I tended to fall asleep while on duty. One Christmas Eve in particular, "Santa" had been trying to blow up a blow-up couch, and he was taking bloody ages! I woke up on the stairs to a red-faced, breathless, mad man, outlining where I had fallen down in the requirements of my new role, to put it politely. Yep, the magic had certainly waned. That's the first part of Christmas.

The second part of Christmas is the day itself, and those wonderful lazy days that link it to New Year's. Niall and I both love the total indulgence of these days. Not for us are the ski slopes of Austria and France; we prefer a glass of wine by the fire with a box of chocolates, and the complete break in our usual routine and from our normal obligations. One meal rolls into another, one cup of tea follows another, the biscuit tin is opened, and the supply of Tayto crisps is steadily depleted.

Now, lest I create a picture of total gluttony and sloth, this is a time for great discussions between Niall and me. The peace that new toys bring! Even so, it is often only after the last of the children have been settled, the house has gone quiet, and the remains of our latest snacks have been cleared that our real conversations take off and go on into the small hours of the morning.

I love these nights; sipping on wine gives us license to go anywhere in the route of our conversations. It is a sweet conductor and a great aid in forming our strategy to conquer the world; though if we have progressed onto the second bottle, our talk usually changes to how we have already conquered the world! A blanket of contentment steals over us, and we are always in agreement with how great we are and how terrific our choices have been. There was no difficulty whatsoever in doing this in the era of the Celtic Tiger, such as it was. Let's face it, just owning your own home made you a millionaire, and it was very easy to be smug.

During Christmas 2001, there was a lot to discuss. After seven long years, having explored all avenues and removed all stones, we finally secured some land adjacent to our home. We wanted to extend our house, and after scaling a sequence of frustrating obstacles, we finally got the green light to go ahead. This marked the beginning of exciting times. We had an architect out before Christmas, and we now had a vision. Our dream was coming true. Dreams cost money, however, and in order to get some, we were forced to look at re-mortgaging our house. These plans constituted much of our conversations that Christmas.

What would the banks allow us? Do we really need to borrow that much? How would this effect the period of our mortgage? Should we extend that too? Could we be plainer in our objectives, or should we just run with the more elaborate ideal? Can we really afford this? These issues overtook us completely, and though absorbing, our conversations were altogether too one-dimensional.

As we were heading toward the end of this wonderful second period of Christmas, during the unique hiatus in time before the cold dawn of January and all that that would bring, we decided to take a break from the heavy conversations of planning, budgeting, and finances. One night, we decided to lighten our evening up a bit, so we talked into the night about the kids, their faces on Christmas morning, how funny their expressions were, their odd questions, and their utter adorability. We may have been into our second bottle of wine by this stage, and the kids were asleep and hence angelic. Thus we classed parenting as a true vocation for which we were rightly chosen. In this candle and liquor imbued atmosphere, I decided to put out a throwaway comment to Niall, a casual conclusion which, in all honesty, I thought would be a mildly humorous interlude. "I suppose our baby days are over?" I asked. I was 33 at the time, Niall was 34. We had three children: two wonderful boys, Adam (6) and Luke (3), and our little girl, Laura (2). We had already given up our twenties, and for the early part of our thirties and beyond we would be pretty much consumed with child rearing. The picture was complete, and our focus was shifting. Or so I thought.

Just as my comment to Niall was a throwaway thing, Niall responded in all sincerity, "Ah no, there's another one in us yet." So much for lightening the conversation! I was amazed. Dumbfounded.

"Are you serious?" I asked him. But already I could feel the claws of excitement in my belly.

"Of course I am," he replied. "I always assumed we'd go again, didn't you? I don't mean straight away, but sometime in the next year or so. What do you think?"

I had no answer.

He continued, "I know, why don't we do what we always do, you come off the pill after New Years, take a break from it for nine months, and by September we can start trying?"

We always tried to have summer babies, hence the September benchmark. Adam was a June baby, Luke was a May baby, but on Laura it didn't quite work—she was conceived only three months into our nine month plan and was thus a January baby, but I didn't like to point this out as I was really warming to the idea. I remember looking at Niall, loving the fact that he was willing to take it all on. Yet, there was a voice in my head asking, "Aren't things pretty much perfect already?"

However, whether it's the Irish Catholic guilt thing in me, coupled with my flying in the face of God by using contraception, I was always very grateful to be able to have children. I heard of so many people having difficulties conceiving, and I very much appreciated my ability to conceive at will. It was almost a duty that because I could have babies, I should have babies. Also, I loved being pregnant, even though I was one of those women who just piled on the weight. But I loved it. Pregnancy was a great state to be in and let's face it, bread, pasta, and sugar donuts were back on the menu!

"Are you serious," I asked him again, putting down my glass of wine and sobering up somewhat. "But what about the build, the finances?" I asked, being uncharacteristically sensible. Now before I go on, let me say this first in deference to my husband. He is a great guy, very sound, and most intelligent. He is the most accommodating guy I know, and he always does right by everybody. But when it comes to having babies, Niall Joye makes absolutely no sense.

So he started along the route of conversation I have heard three times before—experience had taught him nothing.

"Yvonne, the baby won't cost us much to start with."

Here goes...

"Won't you be breastfeeding [*that costs nothing*] and sure nappies aren't really that expensive [*right*], and by the time the baby will cost us money, I'll be earning more money."

Sorted!

Beautiful, just beautiful, and that is how we plan our babies. As I listened to him planning more babies that Christmas night, he reminded me so much of the first time we got pregnant. We were 25 and 26 respectively. We had gotten married the year before, and though I wanted us to start a family straight away, he wanted us to have a year on our own together first. He was so right, though I was a tad put out at the time. By the time our first wedding anniversary dawned, I took my pill packet to him and told him

I would be using it no more. He smiled and said, "Well, let the games begin."

Well, if the games had begun, they weren't much fun. Basically, it didn't happen for us that first month. I couldn't believe it. I really couldn't believe it. There was something wrong with me, and it was all my fault. I deserved it for all the bad things I had ever done, i.e. having sex before marriage, compounded by the add-on sin of using contraception—double whammy! Despite my tendency to bend a few rules every now and then (or break them, as the case may be), Catholicism plays a big role in my life.

I went to the Family Planning Clinic. A young doctor appeared in front of me in the waiting room, and I followed him into his consultancy rooms. He asked me to outline my problem, and even as I spoke I felt childish, impulsive, and very stupid. I explained that I had been on the pill for five years and that I had come off it in June, but now here I was in August, and I was still not pregnant. I told him my cycle was as regular as clockwork, that I knew when my fertile period was, but yet no joy (forgive the pun on the surname).

He stared at me for what seemed like forever, and I felt myself wither in front of him. He rose from his chair, flipped down two charts, and then took what to my mind was a ruler, which he pointed at the first chart.

"This is a chart of what happens to a woman when she is taking contraception, and this," he said, directing his ruler to the second chart, "is a chart of a normal cycle minus contraception."

At this juncture, he turned to me and, with the ruler in his hand, he hopped it between both charts. He asked me, or rather told me, "You have been taking contraception for five years now, yet you want to go from here," the ruler slapped the first chart, "to there," the second chart got a slap, "in just one month?"

I could just hear him thinking, "Are you mad!"

Then he let out a big, big sigh.

"I am so tired of people obsessing about babies. Go home, forget about making babies, and make love to your husband," he counselled me. "If you still have a problem in a year, then we'll talk."

The following month, the same man confirmed my pregnancy.

We took a day off work in honour of our feat and spent it looking at each other incredulously. That day was my first introduction to Niall's thinking on "baby economics". I listened attentively to him as he explained how we were now in a position to net a fortune: we wouldn't be going out as much—money in the bank; I wouldn't be drinking now—a nest egg in the making (Jesus, I don't know how much he thought I drank); and finally, of course, because I wasn't drinking, we now had our very own chauffeur on nights out, so we no longer had to worry about taxis (not that we ever did). He had me convinced. Convinced, but a little hard done by because I could not quite grasp the mad social life he thought we had, or the drinker he thought he had married.

There I was, the one that could work up the equivalent of a small mortgage on my credit card, questioning the economics of things. Niall, the economist, is the solid one, the sane one. Yet, in this one area of life, his reasoning defies logic. Even so, this was always the basis on which we operated when it came to baby making.

And so we left Christmas 2001 with fuller tummies, sore heads, and a jam-packed year planned ahead. We had extensions to build and babies to make. It was big stuff but feck it; we were young and why not! What could possibly go wrong? *What can possibly go wrong?*

3

Money & Sex

Before the good stuff could happen, the practicalities had to be put in place. To build a big new house, we needed money. To produce a fourth cute baby, we needed sex. In the first four months of 2002 we had neither—well nothing of substance in the first instance, or quality in the second. I suppose the money part took us over. It was all about getting the finance in place. Every spare moment we had was taken up with it. We had to get all our bank statements together, we had to list all our outgoings and incomings, get confirmation from Niall's employer of his position, all that stuff. The banks were terrific at approving everything over the phone within 24 hours. There was a big difference, however, between that and getting written approval, and there was a big time lag between the time we received the written approval and getting the cash in our hands. Even when we finally got our written approval, they left us €30,000 short in the written loan offer. That was a major catastrophe.

I went down to the bank to sort this out. The bank clerk was a young fart, asking me farty fecking questions. He started by asking me, "Do you think you could manage without it?"

"Without it?" I replied.

"The 30K," he verified.

Manage without the 30K? Jesus.

I just looked at him. The guy must have been only twenty-something, probably living in a bed-sit with a couch and a portable TV. I guessed he went home every weekend, and the only time he worried about money was when he ran out of it on a Saturday night.

I quelled my frustration and smiled at him. Very politely and very nicely, I brought his attention to the statement of costs we had presented in our original application. I suggested to him that if he looked again, he would find it to be a good indicator as to why we might just need that extra "30K". The expression on his face was like the delayed dawning of day in late December. Apparently, it turned out to be a mere typo, but not before I had suffered heart failure, sleepless nights, and the sexual appetite of a mother of 12.

Interest rates, loan terms, how much more could we stretch ourselves—these were our only preoccupations, and though money is often equated with sex, they were miles apart as far as we were concerned. Waiting to conceive until September was not going to be a problem.

Instead of jumping in the sack as soon as the kids were finally asleep like we used to, (well not quite, but occasionally) we'd get out "the budget" and pour over it. By the time we did get to bed, Niall was exhausted and my head was reeling. I would lie in the bed going over it all in my head, tweaking the budget, then tweaking the plans, visualising, perfecting. Every morning Niall would ask me what changes I had made, and how it would affect the budget. Every day I rang the builder, and he would ask me the same questions. The builder was right up there with my husband, only he might have been ahead in the sex stakes had he been willing to knock a little off the costs!

Things were bad. To make matters worse, we had blown good, decent money on a holiday we could no longer afford. This had been arranged prior to the rollercoaster we now found ourselves on, when we thought we had more money than we actually did, and before we knew the cost of PVC windows, bathroom tiles, lighting, and the rest of it. Lanzarote was our destination of choice and it was booked for mid-May.

As the holiday approached and our guilt mounted because of this unnecessary expenditure, we tried to play around with our options. We couldn't get a refund, and it would be dead money if we decided to opt out. Then we thought, feck it, we'd go. We all needed a holiday, the build was due to get going in July, the timing was good and, anyway, we were this much in debt, why not a little bit more, let's just get excited and go.

Filled with this new optimism and enthusiasm, I logged onto Trip Advisor to check out the accommodation we had booked. Do not ask why I hadn't done this previously! My optimism vanished.

All enthusiasm wilted. It appeared, from all accounts, that our holiday destination was a breeding ground for cockroaches, and the only action between the sheets would be ensuring our shoes remained on our feet and keeping our mouths shut.

I reeled down through the numerous reports. The litany of comments appeared to be more of a guide outlining 50 ways to kill a cockroach than a holiday review. There was no talk of pools, beaches, or even the sun. Everyone who had ever been to this place had apparently been overrun by cockroaches. *Shit!* I was damned if this was going to be our holiday. So the next day, I called the travel agent and outlined our plight. She was impressively accommodating, posing no challenge whatsoever to our change of plan and simply asked that I bear with her whilst she found us an alternative destination. I couldn't believe how easy it all was.

She came back to us a little while later and revealed that the only option available to us was a two week stay in Ibiza. *Ibiza? A haven for lager louts, ladettes, and vodkas at noon. But give me a drunk over a cockroach any day! Ibiza? Home to free and wanton sex—just what we need (albeit tailored to cater for three toddlers)! This holiday will earmark the resurrection of our sex life!* Not that it was dead completely. Of course we had sex in those first few months of 2002—it just wasn't great sex.

We had two scenarios really—gosh that makes it sound interesting; it wasn't. We had the "last thing before sleep" perfunctory session, which was quick and to the point, but suited our exhaustion and stress levels just fine. These couplings were born out of our mutual awareness that we hadn't touched each other for a while, rather than an overwhelming desire to get together. Also, although unspoken, it was important to both of us that we not become a statistic, i.e. one of those married couples who only have sex "X" amount of times a week/month/year. It was a pride thing really.

The second scenario was the "morning glory". Again this sounds better than it was, but it certainly had a lot more going for it. First off, we weren't knackered, well not as knackered. It also had the connotation that we still had it, that we were still mad for each other, that even in the morning we couldn't keep our hands off each other. In truth, however, it lacked the wow factor, which was largely down to the fact that we had three small children downstairs, who might have, at any moment in time, killed themselves, killed each other, or, at the very least, come crashing through the door mid-operandi. With all that going on, the tendency to be innovative didn't have much of a platform. Yep! Ibiza would sort us out properly.

4

Ibiza

Ibiza was beautiful. As the plane lowered itself onto the tarmac of Ibiza's small airport, blue skies, blue seas, and swaying pine trees on rolling hillsides were framed by the small airplane window. A beautiful picture. A wonderful feeling. We were here. Now all we had to do was retrieve our buggies and our baggage, get on the bus, and get to our apartment and the worst part of going on holidays would be over. I think it is the madness that reigns at this juncture that I can't abide. It all becomes a tad uncivilised. I would love to think it a madness that belongs to everyone else, but I must admit, I play my own role.

It always begins in earnest with the frantic retrieval of our hand luggage from the overhead lockers of the plane itself. Those people who are lucky enough to have recovered their own personal belongings with relative ease, are usually of the belief that everyone else should be able to do the same. Not so. And that's how it started with us in Ibiza. As we tried to gather up our three children, our hand luggage, the kids' hand luggage (all of which had been divided and stored within a 5 m radius of our seats), plus the variety of accoutrements that had brought us relative peace on the flight, we encountered a line of passengers waiting "patiently" for us to gather our things. As they continued to wait, and we continued to gather, the line of "patient" people waiting for us to move felt more like a firing squad, albeit with fake smiles and forced politeness. *What is the fucking rush?* And then the race to the baggage hall began.

I suppose I really should have more appreciation for people's anxiety to get to the baggage reclaim as fast as possible because my first-born son Adam suffers from a similar strain of the "virus" and is always very keen to be a part of the race. Even at the age of six, he had somehow grasped the urgency of the situation, and it was not for him to be associated with a family of stallers. So, as we endeavoured to manoeuvre our three-year-old and two-year-old through the aisle of the plane and down the stairway, Adam was off, already in step with the marathon pace of everyone else. At the bottom of the plane's steps, on the melting tarmac, we unfolded the buggies. Heavy bags were dragging from our shoulders, bottles were being located, and babies were resisting repositioning. All the time, we were feigning smiles and gently calling for Adam to slow up.

"Adam, come back, come back please Adam." We really didn't want to have to shout, but Adam just ignored us.

Shite!

"Adam, come back honey, come back, you'll get lost!" We were still not quite shouting, but we were certainly more forceful.

Why won't Luke just sit still in the buggy while I secure the belt?

"Get back here Adam, get back here now!" this time it was a bona fide shout.

For God's sake Luke, just sit still! I felt drops of perspiration on my forehead.

"Niall, get Adam, we'll lose him," I urged.

"I haven't Laura's belt on," he replied, fumbling with the straps as any amount of bags slipped from his shoulders.

It is so fecking hot!

"Leave it, I'll get that, just bring him back," I yelled at him.

Go!

Niall dropped everything and ran. I pulled all our bits and pieces together and, balancing it with the two toddlers, who were now locked into the buggies [*thank God*], I too jumped into the race, becoming just like all the other mad eejits, competing for the prize of our luggage, and hopefully the recapture of our son. Niall retrieved Adam, but he was heaving, indignant, and most verbal—the seeds had been sown for the first tantrum of the holiday. We ignored it.

We were now into the second stage of this torturous process—getting our bags off the carousel. *Fun and games!* Adam saw the carousel as his first holiday introduction to the funfair and, therefore, insisted on riding it, surfing it—anything but stand next to it. We tried to discreetly coax him off the belt, with no success. Then our coaxing became a loving but firm instruction, to which he paid absolutely no heed. Invariably, the scene concluded with us grabbing him roughly, pulling him towards us, and gripping his hand tightly enough to let him know that we meant business—then we had the full blown hissy fit. Guilt overwhelmed us and a back-up lollipop was produced to quell the storm, staying the calamity for a little while longer, at least where Adam was concerned. Our peace token to Adam had inadvertently created a mutiny in the two buggies, but the other two children were too young to have a lollipop, so I searched for something else with which to pacify them: bottles, keys, plastic toys, anything at all. Everything I chose, however, ended up being thrown and spewed across the polished tiles of the terminal building. *Feck this anyway!* Then I felt the original offending lollipop being shoved and squashed into the palm of my hand. Adam had spied the first suitcase emerging through the fringe on the carousel.

"I want to help Dad get the bags," he cried, and the cycle began again.

Terrific! On top of all of this, I started to have a panic attack. I always have a disproportionate fear of losing our luggage, and my prayers commenced: *Please God, don't let our bags be lost, please. Please, God, let them come through, please!* Then came the questions: *What will we do if one of the suitcases doesn't make it? What way did I pack? Which suitcase can we do without?* You'd think that because of this phobia, I would learn to pack each suitcase in a manner that would temporarily meet all our needs. I never do.

I tried to calm myself down by pulling the buggies well clear of the belt and removing myself from the cut-throat business that was going on there. I distracted myself with my two now overtly and piercingly impatient babies, who were bursting to break free from their confines. In the midst of this chaos (which invited its fair share of spectators), I couldn't resist my gaze being dragged to the unfolding events at the carousel. Adam was back up riding it again, and one of our bags had come through. *At least we got one.* Niall, however, had run into trouble. He had tried to drag both Adam and the bag off together, but had found no space to land either. He glared at me through the bodies of the baggage retrieval mob, as though by some shagging miracle I could sort it all out. *Fucking typical!*

So I ploughed through the crowds, "Sorry, sorry, sorry," leaving my two shrieking babies behind me. I grabbed and hoisted Adam off Niall, returned to the fold, and confronted the newly totalled three bawling children I had before me. *Just beautiful!* I glanced over at Niall. He was happy now. *And why not?* In typical male fashion, he had only one thing to do, retrieve the bags, while I was looking around trying to ascertain where I might change into my Wonder Woman outfit! Just as I felt nerves and sweat glands beginning to explode with the pressure of maintaining a dignified composure in the face of so many onlookers, I saw Niall coming towards us, pushing a trolley. Every single case was accounted for, and the feeling of relief that enveloped me was almost orgasmic. *Not that I remember how that feels.*

Now, only one more level left in the game—the bus journey. We emerged from the deceptive coolness of the airport building back into the furnace that existed outside. Our travel guide, a beautiful girl, immaculately dressed, without a bead of sweat, and lips slashed red to match the red scarf at her neck, smiled indulgently at us, five bedraggled individuals. She told us in her lovely Northern English accent that our bus was the No. 18. We returned fake smiles and plodded forward, squinting against the sunlight, too tired to locate our sunglasses, and too busy surveying the line of buses before us. Ignoring all childish requests, grievances, and demands, we walked past row upon row of buses. Their engines were on at full throttle, and the fumes funnelled down our throats while the heat blasted onto our faces. We eventually reached the No. 18 and were told where to load our luggage. The babies had to be uprooted from their buggies—heaven for them, more complications for us. I grabbed and held all three children close to me, paying no attention to the violent efforts they were each making to break free. Niall got to load on the bags while I felt I was in a chain-gang—check-in bags, retrieve bags, load bags, offload bags, so on, and so on. *I wanna get off!*

We boarded the bus and searched for seats where we could all sit together. It seemed we were the last to arrive, and everyone else appeared to be so calm, so quiet, so together, and so impossibly cool. *Where are all the families with kids?* The atmosphere in the darkened bus was almost sophisticated with its hushed conversations and muted lighting. Of course, we blew all that out of the water with our three wailing children. To find space for all of us, we had to go to the back of the bus. It was whilst en route there that I got the unmistakable whiff off my youngest—going on holiday mid-toilet training is not a good idea. I told myself that no one else could probably smell it and was prepared to live with the guilt of having her sit in it. That is until my two verbal older boys, with all the tact of a dog in heat, simultaneously suspended their tantrums and declared to all and sundry that "Laura has a smelly". They then proceeded to fall about the place laughing at having said the exact same thing at the exact same time. *Great! Friends at last.* I had no other choice but to acknowledge, by way of an apologetic smile, that indeed we had a problem.

After doing the dastardly deed as inconspicuously as possible, and in the tightest of confines (whilst Niall tried to deal with the boys who were verging on extreme hyperactivity), I emerged from the bus in a desperate attempt to offload the offending article. I ran back along the line of overheated buses before I finally found what I was looking for. I dumped the pullup, took a deep breath, and ran back to face the music. My body was drenched in sweat. When I eventually returned to the bus, the impatience of our fellow passengers was palpable. Nobody said anything, of course, but I could sense their frustration in their body language and in their eyes. Christ, their eyes alone could have taken me out.

Niall must have given the boys the bribe of their lives because they appeared to be quiet now, suspiciously munching on something that I am sure was ordinarily totally forbidden. *I really don't give a fuck.* Smelling beautiful, Laura turned back into the sweet creature that she is. I sat down next to Niall, and Laura climbed into my arms. She was sleepy. *Thanks be to God.* I glanced over at Niall, his handsome face was drawn, his forehead was patterned with droplets of sweat, and his wonderful blue eyes were dull with exhaustion. I slipped my sticky hand into his sticky hand and squeezed it, but he didn't return the gesture. I knew then that romance and making love, let alone making babies, was the furthest thing from his mind.

The bus journey was surprisingly short and unbelievably calm. It was almost 6 p.m. by the time the coach pulled up in front of our apartment complex, and though the temperature of the day was still intense, the sting was less so. Our emergence back into the Ibizan air was not as drastic as I had anticipated. There was the usual queue to check-in, but it ran smoothly, and we found ourselves on the top floor of an attractive, whitewashed, low-rise apartment block. It was a big apartment, very spacious, with an impressive roof terrace affording us wonderful views of the beach and the pools below.

Niall brought the kids down to the pool while I unpacked the bags. I found places for everything and tried to make a home of the place. I opened the French doors and walked out onto the roof terrace. I saw Niall and the kids below splashing in the pool, and the awfulness of the previous few hours evaporated. Suddenly, having our kids with us on holiday made perfect sense.

We had only one neighbour. I could see their towels, swimsuits, and goggles all laid out to dry, and from the items thrown on the terrace, chiefly a giant blow-up dolphin, they appeared to have kids. Nobody was there, but I thought we might meet them later in the evening and, perhaps, the boys could make a friend.

Niall and the kids returned to the apartment wet, happy, and hungry. We dressed and set out for our first meal of the holiday. The evening was perfection personified. The whole ambience had changed and, finally, as a family we seemed to rhyme.

The first sip of holiday wine is always the sweetest, and the unmistakable whiff of garlic a great reminder of all that is good about sun holidays. As we sat on the terrace of the restaurant surrounded by lush bougainvillea, it was difficult to believe we were actually there, unpacked, and finally relaxing. I looked to Niall, and I saw the first signs of him unwinding, not quite there yet, but getting there. Seeing him in his white t-shirt, shorts, and with a beer in hand, he really did look the part. I envisaged us returning to the apartment, getting the kids settled, having a drink on the terrace, falling into bed, and finally watering the drought that had reigned in our love life. And so it all came to pass, except that is for that last part. He was too tired! *Wonderful!*

The kids were terrific. Exhausted by the excitement, the journey, and their record breaking tantrums, they fell to sleep very quickly. We tiptoed out to the terrace, me with a glass of wine, Niall with a beer. Thankfully, the neighbours weren't home yet, and everything was as it had been previously. We were finally alone. Our conversation, however, was all one-sided. My side. Niall was quiet and contributed very little. For a while, I tried to ignore the imbalance but, tiring, I accepted defeat.

"You're knackered, aren't you?" I asked him. For the first time that day, he smiled, a real genuine smile, but one that had a hint of a forthcoming apology. I was right.

"I'm sorry, Yvonne, I really am, but I've just hit a wall. I really need some sleep." he said. Then he paused and added as an afterthought, "Though it is nice sitting here, listening to you." He only said that so I wouldn't get miffed.

"Go on," I said. "In fairness, we've had a mad day. Sure we have two weeks for talking and everything else," betraying a little of what my intentions had been for the night. He looked over at me for a few seconds as if still debating what he should do, until I made the choice for him. "Go on," I said again. "I'd actually enjoy a little peace here on my own. I'll stay out here a little longer, and I'll be in to you then."

He got up, came over to me, and returned the squeeze I had given him on the bus. Before he went through to the bedroom, he leaned down and kissed me full on the mouth. *You can't do that to me!* As I sat there, I hoped the people next door wouldn't return as I was now enjoying the solitude. It was nice that warm evening, sitting there, looking up at starry skies, hearing the strains of music from distant bars and voices from passers-by at the poolside below. The moon was illuminated on the sea. I felt good.

It was perhaps a good thing that Niall and I didn't indulge that night. I was coming up to my fertile period and nearing the end of my safe period. Whenever I was off the pill, I became very good at recognising the signs. I did debate going back on the pill for our holiday, just so we could park all that for a while and throw caution to the wind, but with all that was going on, I never got round to it.

Absently, I wondered where the people from next door were. They must have gone on a day excursion with a late return. Perhaps their holiday was over and they had merely left their gear behind. In that case, we might hop over and take the dolphin in the morning. I still don't fully understand my preoccupation with our temporary neighbours' activities. Generally we keep to ourselves on holidays. With Adam getting older, however, I liked the idea of him having a little holiday buddy. I thought it might make things a little more interesting for him.

Suddenly I felt the events of the day overtake me. Combined with the heat and the wine, I fell into bed. I appreciated the black out curtains on the French doors and the inky blackness of the room. I lay alongside Niall and promptly fell asleep.

The voices, though loud and harsh, did not wake me immediately. I was having such a lovely dream, but now it was clouded by shouting and profanities. I wanted to keep on dreaming, but the voices were winning. I willed myself to open my eyes. I wanted rid of the noises. When I did finally open my eyes, it was difficult to know if, in fact, I had opened them. The room was pitch-dark. I couldn't make out anything. For a few moments, I had no idea where I was. I couldn't get my bearings, and I had to shift myself in the bed to make sure I was awake, that the dream was indeed over.

Gradually, my eyes adjusted to the darkness and shapes came into focus. I re-familiarised myself with the room. Ibiza—apartment. *Ah yes.* I knew where I was. It had been the voices that had confused me because, just as it took me sometime to emerge from my sleep, I finally realised that the voices, the shouts, and the insults were not part of any dream, but very much a reality in the adjoining apartment. Clearly, our neighbours had returned.

It was some argument. Insults were hurtled. Profanities flowed. Furniture was pushed. A plate broke. I had never before heard such coldness and so much hate in a set of voices. I was frozen in the bed. I sensed Niall was awake beside me, but I didn't look at him, nor did I say anything because I was clinging to the weak hope that I was still dreaming. I felt very small in the bed; similar, I imagine, to how a child must feel when caught between feuding parents.

It was as if I had willed it. The next thing I heard was a child's voice crying, "Mummy, mummy!" A little boy. A little boy crying. The argument was escalating, ultimatums were given, and the little boy's cries grew shriller. Finally, a door slammed and there was silence. *Silence.* After what seemed an infinity, I turned to Niall. In the shadows, I could see his lashes blinking. He was definitely awake.

"God, Niall did you hear all that?" I whispered.

"I did," he replied.

"Should we do something?" I asked him, still whispering.

"Like what?" he returned. Niall can be a bit too in-tune with the harshness of life some times.

"We can't just lie here; did you hear the little boy? Did you hear him, Niall? He was in an awful state," I said, speaking louder now.

Niall sighed.

"Yvonne, there is nothing to do. It's done. It's finished. I'm sure they'll be embarrassed in the morning. They probably had a day like us only drank too much. Leave it be," he informed me, as though he had the inside track.

"God, Niall I don't know; I don't know," I replied, incredulous.

Of course now that the power of speech had returned to me in full throttle, and in order to make sense of it all for myself, I launched into a litany of the vagaries of life and debated, again largely to myself, the whys and ifs of it all. By the end of my tirade, we were both wide awake. In the absence of any further rumblings from next door, I began to relax and accept Niall's argument that it was most likely drink related, and though it was unfortunate to have the little boy privy to it, they were now most probably all wrapped up, happy in bed. I didn't believe that last bit. *That poor little boy.*

My mind was all over the place, and I couldn't quite believe it when I felt Niall slip his hand up my thigh. *He can't be in the mood?* He then began to nuzzle my neck and lifted his other hand to my breast. *I love it when he does that, but seriously...* He then started biting my ear. That sets me off every time. I gave into it. After all the tension, I released myself, and we fell into each other. For the first time in a long time, we made love as opposed to just grabbing an opportunity for sex.

The next morning I went to the bathroom. I had a familiar discharge, and I knew we had just made our fourth baby. I knew it would be a little boy.

Lost in deep thought and silent (for once), I went out onto the terrace, the bright sunlight denied the events of the previous night, and I looked across to the neighbouring terrace. All signs of life were gone: the swimsuits, the goggles, and so too the blow-up dolphin. I was glad he had been able to take it with him.

5

The Cork Question

Now, as if we didn't have enough going on in our lives, we did have one further complication during our holiday. Niall's job. In the past, Niall had been headhunted by several medical companies, an area in which he had worked for the past number of years. Up until then, however, there had been no offers which he entertained seriously. The latest approach had come in the weeks preceding our holiday in May and, unlike other instances, this opportunity seemed to capture him.

Coming up to our holiday, he had a series of meetings with various representatives of the organisation looking to recruit him. They flew him to the UK and showed him around their headquarters, where he met with some further significantly placed people. He was low key about it and remained non-committal in our conversations, yet I sensed something about this job was ticking his boxes. On the eve of our trip to Ibiza, they offered him the position. They told him they didn't want to pressurise him, so they asked that he consider the offer over his holiday and revert to them upon his return. This was great as it gave us ample time to consider our options—the only thing was, with all that was going on, it was difficult to find the mind space for that kind of decision.

In short, it was a terrific offer. It was significantly more money, the company products were superior, and he could expect to have more autonomy in his role. It would make the increase in our mortgage more comfortable, and it would open up whole new avenues of work that appealed to him. You'd imagine, this would have been a simple choice. A no-brainer, as they say. The problem, however, was timing. And me. It was all too unfamiliar. When faced with the financial outlay we were about to embark on, security, rather than buckets of money, was my preferred option. Even though we might be more comfortably well-off on this new venture, I couldn't help wondering whether it would be short-lived and what would happen if it didn't work out. What if in the long term the position proved to be unstable?

Okay, so we were being ultra conservative. I was being ultra conservative, but Niall had been with his job for five years by then, and it was a good company, with a solid background, and he was treated well. Job security is not a bad thing—it might not light up your world, but at least you can make realistic plans. If we were to take on all the projects we had planned and set about spending the money we were about to spend, we needed to feel safe and, frankly, the status quo felt safe. So believe it or not, the night before we took off to Ibiza, we agreed that this was not the time for this job. Done, decision made.

Niggle, niggle, niggle.

Niall then asked that we not talk about it during the holiday, and we didn't. That is until about three days before we were due to return, and it was Niall who brought it up.

Surprise!

We were sitting outside another quaint restaurant (every restaurant in Ibiza was quaint), it was a balmy evening (every night was balmy), and everything was just so pleasant. I cannot remember where the kids were but, obviously, they must have been with us, though all I can remember is us getting into a conversation and being allowed to follow it through to the end.

"I've been thinking about the job, Yvonne," Niall told me. I didn't say anything—I can shut up sometimes. "You know, I've been thinking," he continued. "This is really an opportunity for us. Maybe it's a gamble, but not a stupid one, and it would mean…" and he proceeded to list all that he found exciting about the post. I listened as he talked and talked. He became animated and almost boyish in the expression of his feelings. I didn't interrupt him, nor was I tempted to. All that he was saying was a revelation to me, and I needed to hear it. I needed to stop my planning, my balancing act, and my playing it safe and really listen to the man. His thoughts, obviously built up over the previous 10 days, came spilling out. There I was, believing that Roy Keane and the furore in Saipan were the only things occupying his mind that holiday—I was mistaken. He had been doing a lot of thinking.

After unloading all his thought processes, he looked at me and asked simply, "So, what do you think?"

I paused, before responding with a question: "If you weren't married Niall and you didn't have three kids…" I nearly mentioned the fourth, but stopped myself just in time, "and you weren't planning an extension, would you take this job?"

Without hesitation he answered, "Yes."

"There's your answer then."

And just like that, we had a whole new plan. Only this time, it was Niall who took centre stage. To see the world of his career opening up in his eyes and to hear the enthusiasm in his voice, I felt immense guilt that I hadn't until that moment registered just how bored he had become and how restless he was to progress. Just as I was in the process of beating myself up, he came out with one of those (dangerous) throwaway comments that get us into so much trouble.

"You know, this means we could move back to Cork!"

Cork? Cork? Move back to Cork? That had come out of the blue, and the thought actually winded me. *What in God's name does Cork have to do with any of this?*

"What?" I asked him. "Are you serious?" I looked at him closely and asked, "What do you mean?"

"I never mentioned it before," he replied, "but when I met with the guys in London they said that I could base myself anywhere in the country. Anywhere. Think about it Yvonne; before we go down the path of the extension and all that crap in July, we could look instead at moving, get a seriously nice house in Cork for a lot cheaper. We'd have none of the hassle of the build. Nice eh? What do you think? It's worth a thought, isn't? It is worth a thought!"

Worth a thought. Worth a thought? God that's an understatement! For years it was all we had ever thought about. For five years it had been all I had ever thought about. Cork was home. Cork was where we came from. Cork was where our story began. But that was many years ago. That was before Dublin got under our skin, before we had three children who spoke with Dublin accents, before we set up a real home, with real friends, and a real sense of belonging. I was speechless. *Cork?*

I looked at him then, across the table in Ibiza, tanned and lean. I always think I am married to someone else in the summer. Not that he looks bad in winter, but he is a real boy of the summer. I think I love him so much that way because that is how he looked when I first laid eyes on him. In Cork. In August 1987.

He had just returned from Ocean City, New Jersey, after working for the summer on a JI visa. He came back with the inflated ego of a guy who had spent the summer in the company of girls who wanted nothing other than to bag an Irish boyfriend. He had been busy!

I, on the other hand, was all grown up, working in an office located on the Grand Parade, around the corner from the South Mall in Cork. I had revolted against family tradition and refused to go to university immediately after leaving school in 1986.

I wanted to "explore my options" as I put it to my father. My father, in no uncertain terms, told me I could do all the "exploring" I wanted, just so long as I accompanied it with a "good decent secretarial course", so that first year after finishing school, I enrolled in the Cork School of Commerce and learned to type and take shorthand. From there, I secured a terrific little number in Bord Fáilte, (or the Irish Tourist Board as it was known then), and as the fourth child of five, I was the only one bringing money into the house other than my father, who was now a major fan of my whole "exploring" notion.

So when Niall and I first met, we were very different people. Yet we were going in the same direction. Having done my stint in the big world, I decided I wasn't yet ready for it and returned to academia. I enrolled in a course in UCC in October of 1987, studying German and Sociology. This, of course, was much to the confusion of my father, who had fully embraced the fact that I had leap-frogged into the working world. Suddenly, reverting to form and following my siblings to university, left him somewhat under-whelmed.

As it turned out, Niall and I used to meet quite often whilst cycling into college. We also happened to both take a part-time job in Dunnes Stores to help pay our fees. Niall's American ego had waned and underneath it emerged a sincere guy with no particular agenda except to seek out my company. That was nice. I was quietly falling for him. He never made a move, however; he never touched me, never even made an innuendo. He was an unknown entity to me and didn't reveal his cards until one night in November 1987.

It was a Monday night. A very cold night. I answered the front door of my house to find him leaning against his bicycle. *Why is he here?* He asked if he could come in. Surprised, but maintaining my cool, I led him through to our "good room", past the glass door of the front room where my entire family (two brothers, two sisters, and two parents) were gathered watching TV. He sat down, comfortable as you like, and started to talk about nothing in particular. It was just like the conversations we had had a dozen times before, always enjoyable but nothing urgent. *Why in God's name is he here?*

There was a knock on the door. It was my Dad. *Oh Jesus!* He had the full silver service out which he promptly brought in, saying we must be dying for a cup of tea. *Ah God, Dad!* Left with no other option, I introduced them and proceeded to observe Niall's interaction with my father. It was nice to have the space to assess him in this new situation. He was at ease, confident in himself, and seemed genuinely pleased to meet my father. My father was doing a little assessing of his own. He observed Niall closely: clean clothes, clean fingernails, good teeth, good diction, and a diamond stud in his left earlobe (a gift from a rich American girl during the summer). When Dad finally left us, I thought Niall might just bolt for the door, thankful for a narrow escape. But he didn't. He stayed.

Finally, he let the small talk die down, and after a pause he said, "I'm just going to say this… I'd like for you to become my girlfriend."

Oh my God.

Gone was the slickness and cockiness of the summer; in its place was a regular guy doing the most regular of things. Only it felt anything but regular.

"How would you feel about that?" he asked, more nervous now.

How would I feel about that? I'd feel great about that. Keep cool though, keep cool.

"Yeah, that would be nice; yeah I would like that," I answered and, suddenly, I was smiling for Ireland and couldn't wipe the fecking grin off my face. There was a moment of silence.

"So what does this mean?" I asked him, still smiling. He was smiling now too, but not quite as stupidly as me.

"I dunno," he answered honestly, and I don't think it really mattered to him now that he had gotten the words out. "I suppose we might meet once or twice a week or something?" he suggested

"Yeah, okay," I answered. "That'd be nice."

We were silent again for a moment, and I was still fecking smiling. The tension was palpable. I felt awkward.

"Right then; I suppose I should be off," he said.

I finally stopped smiling. *Jesus, he's right; otherwise Dad'll be in with a hot drop!* We both got up, and I walked him out the hall, past the glass door again and the six sets of eyes, through the front door, and around to our side passage where he had propped up his bike. It was cold and, though he had his coat on,

I was only wearing a shirt. He drew me to him and, officially now my boyfriend, he felt justified in leaning in and seeking out my lips. I met him half way and the seal of our new relationship was imminent. The kiss… was a disaster. A shambles. It was all over the place. Yet I felt great. He must have felt good about it too because as he cycled off into the night, he shouted back, "Can I see you tomorrow night?"

"You can," I shouted back and right there and then was our beginning. The business of meeting once or twice a week never took off; we never spent a day apart, which gave us plenty of time to perfect and master the kissing and a whole lot more besides.

We were a pretty tight couple all through college. We went to the States in the summer of 1988, bought a car for $350, and drove from New York to Florida. The following summer, in 1989, I went to Germany, and he went back to the States, but it was like we were never apart. We discovered letter writing, which introduced a whole new dimension to our relationship.

By the time we left college in 1990, Ireland was still clambering to get out of the recession of the 1980s. There were few jobs going, and neither Niall nor I held much hope of securing work in Ireland, let alone Cork. The Donnelly Visas for the States were on offer at the time, but we failed to secure them; although hope was generated with the promise of the Morrison Visa being introduced, but that was not going to be for some time yet.

For the first six months after graduating, Niall worked in an off licence, and I worked as a secretary in my father's office, which pleased Dad enormously as no one else in the family had shown any interest in working in the family firm. Dad and I had a real see-saw relationship when it came to my professional life. During this time, Niall and I applied for every potential opportunity that we came across, and I was living in dread of the day either one of us would secure something, as it would certainly mean separation. We were so wrapped up in each other that life without being in the shadow of one another held no appeal. Yet we were realistic. We knew we needed to get our careers off the ground and that we were too young to hold each other back.

In December 1990, our day of reckoning arrived. I got a position in a software company in Dublin that needed an administrator who spoke German. New Year's Day 1991 saw me leaving home, leaving Niall, and beginning life anew—alone. Up until that point, that was the worst day of my life. It poured rain incessantly, and I cried the whole way to Dublin.

Niall joined me three weeks later. He had no job and no income, but we were together again. Feck holding each other back! We were much happier holding onto each other. We found an apartment in Rathmines, moved in together, and our adult life began. Within a month, Niall had secured a position as a financial adviser, which afforded us a nice shiny company car and, though he hated the job, at least we had the outward trappings of a couple who were moving forward in their lives. We went grocery shopping like proper adults, put our joint names on things like electricity and telephone bills, and we got to lie in the same bed every night. I loved that. We had the freedom of being adults, but were childlike in the novelty of it.

After that first year, however, our priorities caught up with our ages and we became more serious in our plans. We decided that we wanted to return to Cork. However, retaining the fringe benefits of independence that Dublin afforded us, would be no small feat in Cork. As Niall pointed out, if we did return to Cork, it wouldn't be as easy for us to live together as it had been in Dublin. It would be expected that we would return to our respective folds and, all in all, that would most certainly be a backward step for us.

Over a cold pizza and a new budget plan, Niall suggested we get married, that we set a wedding date, and co-ordinate our job search in Cork around that date. There it was: my marriage proposal, in a kitchen in Rathmines, born out of budgets and Catholic family morals. It involved neither Paris, nor a diamond ring but, to date, it has been the best offer I have ever received.

We were getting married. The date we agreed was 26 June 1993, and though our resources were building up, it was difficult to see it happening. We told no one as we went ahead and booked photographers, bands, venues, the church, and the priest ("Are ya sure about this now cos I have young ones all the time with love bites on their necks asking me 'Father, will you marry us, Father, will ya?'"). I found it all to be a great hoot, but totally surreal. It was like playing grown-up. That was until one day in October 1992, when Niall suggested we go look for a ring because he really wanted to let everyone know that I had agreed to become his wife.

Funny, as life took over, Cork became a little less important. We still applied for all and sundry with Niall even receiving letters from companies he hadn't known he'd applied to (I was always very enthusiastic on his behalf), but unbeknownst to us, we were creating our new normality and finding new parameters. We were discovering pleasures other than "the craic" in Cork, and we were becoming a family to each other.

The planned return to Cork never materialised, but the wedding in June did. The sweetest part of it all was that now, no matter where we lived, or where we'd end up, we would always go together and stay together, bringing us back to the balmy night in Ibiza, a decade on from all those failed attempts at returning to Cork, and now this boy made good was giving me a second chance at our original dream.

We talked into the night, giggling about where we would live, what schools the kids would go to, and how our families would react. We fell into bed drunk on the notion of it all.

I awoke the next morning and turned to Niall, who was already awake. I told him honestly that my dream was no longer Cork. The dream was us, him and me, our three kids (I still hadn't said anything about the fourth), and a blueprint for an extension to a three-bedroom-semi in Ballinteer.

He turned to me and smiled. "Well thanks be to Jesus for that!" He hadn't slept all night from worrying about how he would break the same news to me. We had a morning glory moment right there and then, and it certainly lived up to its name.

6

Silk Stockings and No Breakfast!

On our return from Ibiza, I got confirmation of what I already knew—I was pregnant. We were expecting our fourth baby, and it was due on Valentine's Day, 2003. Niall was thrilled. The fast track on the plan didn't put him out at all; on the contrary, he was convinced that this was turning out much better than the original plan. The way he viewed it, we had two projects: the pregnancy and the build. The build would be a four month project, finishing by November, decorated by mid-December, home and dry for Christmas, with a fully feathered nest by February, all timed beautifully for the conclusion of our second project: the baby. As far as Niall was concerned, this should have been the plan from the start.

It was all rhyming—Niall's job (along with the extension) was to commence in July. This suited me just fine as it would place me firmly in the role of project manager right from the get-go—a role I had coveted from the fledging stage of the whole endeavour. Niall's energies had to be directed towards establishing himself in his new role, and I was most eager to relieve him of any misguided notions that he could manage both aptly. No, this belonged to me and just as Niall saw two projects, I saw two babies, the one I was carrying and the one I was building.

There was no denying that it was a big project. We had a three-bedroom semi-detached house, but we intended to double its size. We did not necessarily want a whole lot more rooms, but a whole lot more space. Our aim was to enlarge all the existing rooms rather than create extra rooms, and we intended to do this by moving the staircase and the front door, thereby increasing the living room, the kitchen, and the hallways, as well as adding two new bedrooms upstairs.

In retrospect, we were naive in our approach; simplistic even. We assumed we could live in situ throughout all the upheaval. I can't even remember us ever sitting down and thinking through the actual day-to-day logistics of living in a building site. We never considered the dirt, the noise, and the urine splashes of strangers on the toilet seat. We were prepared to rough it and rise above it. We thought it noble that we were being so cost efficient and budget conscious. We felt we were being stoic because we were prepared to meet it all head on, in a practical and nonsensical fashion.

The truth was much blander. We had to put up with it because, quite simply, we didn't have the money to do otherwise. Finding accommodation for the duration of the renovations was simply a cost too far. It was a mistake; my mistake. It was born of my longing for instant gratification and involved me glossing over the necessary banalities to achieve our ultimate goal. I was coming from the new school of thought that believed it was possible to have everything you wanted, and afford none of it. Silk stockings and no breakfast!

We did have to make budgetary allowances for the designer kitchen "that could not be imitated", the obligatory marble floors that were "the staple diet of any decent extension", and if temporary harsh living arrangements meant we could then proceed with ordering the intricate mosaic tiles we would "enjoy for the rest of lives" (which I now can't stand), then it would all be worth it—absolutely. The false economies that became my sound bites, and my blind ambition to have it all, meant we would just have to do without a safe, functioning, clean home environment for six months. *What's six months in the greater scheme of things?* Indeed.

Well, two months down the line, the hammering grew louder, the excavator turned more aggressive and, at every mealtime, the tray on Laura's highchair accumulated a brand new layer of fresh dust. It had been fine to start with, exciting even, with the kids boasting of their very own Bob the Builder (in a variety of sizes and shapes!). Back walls came crashing down to squeals of laughter from the three children pressed against the glass of the "viewing gallery", i.e. our bedroom. Hard hats were borrowed and lunch boxes packed in preparation for their new vocations as builders. It was good clean fun and wasn't it great to add it to their repertoire of childhood memories?

Great, until September that is, when things started going wrong in more ways than one.

By the time September rolled in, the building work was getting closer to the perimeters of the house. The builders and their digging machines had lost their novelty, and the distinctive autumnal feel of leaving the lighter days of summer behind to face the growing gloom of winter, tinged our mood slightly. None of this was helped by the often hazardous conditions in which we found ourselves, and there was a growing, definite, and almost eerie sense that our home was no longer ours. *We ain't in Kansas anymore!*

"We have to move out," I told Niall one evening.

"We can't!" came his expected reply.

Jesus, if only we had more money.

We spent more nights pouring over spreadsheets, trying to find a way. We simply couldn't do it. We could not afford extra rent on top of the increased mortgage payments which we were now repaying. Stupidly, we had already drawn down on the new mortgage. It had just seemed easier to do it that way, and the bank had been great about it! *We're trapped, and it's all my fault!* My guilt wasn't enough to stop me wanting everything that was itemised in the budget, however, despite the sum of their total.

"The taps need to be chrome," I repeated. "It has to be those door handles, it just has to be!"

I considered going to my parents' house in Cork, but I knew we couldn't really. Adam was in school now, and Luke was in prepaid Montessori. *We really didn't think this one through!* We had to stay. I had to stay! *This is my baby.* Nevertheless, it wasn't taking shape quite the way we had planned it. Life imitating life! I made some mistakes along the way, and one big one in particular.

We were building a sunroom onto the back of the house. Ignoring advice from my husband, the builders, and the architects (they all blurred into one on some occasions), I wanted a sunroom with a twist. It had to be different from the thousands I had seen before. To achieve this, I wanted the back wall to be a wall of natural stone with a fire inserted but no windows. Plenty of light would stream through the glass walls on the sides and through the Velux window in the roof. The idea was that, on entering the room, you would be welcomed by this modern "fire in the wall" feature, beautifully offset against the "expert masonry" employed in the natural brick wall. *Beautiful, terrific, and it was all my idea!* The plan was that it would be quite at odds with common expectations of a sunroom, and it certainly was.

One Sunday morning, with the dew still covering the various new shapes surrounding the shell of our original home, Niall and I stepped into the skeleton of this sunroom. Rubble formed the floor, and a sharp wind blew at us through the two open sides where the windows and French doors would eventually go. It was a cold morning in late September, the roof was not yet in place, and the dark grey sky above us held the promise of unloading its burden.

Niall wasn't looking at any of this. He stood in the middle of the space in his boxers and a well worn T-shirt that would not have been out of place when he worked the Boardwalk in New Jersey, all those years ago. He kept staring at the blank wall that stood in the middle of our garden. It was our sunroom wall, out of place for now, and without its eventual connections and adornments to give it context. I was jabbering on about what would go where, trying to get my sense of space and putting words to the vision that was in my head. I was just about to pinpoint the movement of the sun when I heard him ask, "Yvonne, can you please tell me why in God's name we can no longer see our garden?"

I just looked at him. I followed his gaze, and I looked at the solid windowless wall before us. I had no answer.

"Isn't the idea of a sunroom supposed to be that you get to semi-live in your garden?" he continued reasonably, never taking his eyes off the wall. Our very own squash court.

I still had no answer. *He's right. Shit.* We both stood there staring at the dark, newly-built backside of our future home. The first drops of rain began to fall, and it no longer mattered what way the fucking sun was shining. I got it wrong. *Shit, fucking, shit.*

"Will I ring Dave?" I finally managed to ask. Dave was our builder.

"It's a Sunday, give the guy a break, Yvonne," Niall replied tiredly.

"Niall, I won't relax until I know he can fix it," I urged impatiently. *I WANT IT NOW!*

He looked up at the sky. The rain was coming down heavy now. *That T-shirt really has seen better days.* He was resigned.

"Whatever Yvonne, whatever," he said as he moved wearily towards the house.

I ran after him.

"I'll fix it Niall. I'll talk to Dave. We'll make it right," I assured him. "I got it wrong. I just got it wrong, Niall. I'm going to ring Dave now. I can't wait; I'll fix it!"

We fixed it alright, fixed it beautifully—for another two grand. But hey I was happy; wasn't that all that mattered? I just couldn't let things go. I couldn't just make do. I had to have everything the way I wanted it, regardless of cost. It had to be perfect. *Is it because I'm pregnant? Is that why I'm being like this? Am I imbalanced? Am I being unreasonable and suffering from tunnel vision as a result?* I knew the answers to all these questions, and my pregnancy had nothing to do with it. It was all about me getting my dream and getting it at whatever price. I'd become a monster, albeit an exhausted monster. *Could I blame exhaustion?* I was definitely exhausted, but I wasn't sure whether that was down to my workload or the pregnancy. I couldn't remember being so tired on a pregnancy before. It was overwhelming. It was worrying and wasn't helped by that September visit to our doctor and the irregular heartbeat of our baby. I was an exhausted and worried monster.

October came round and conditions in the house deteriorated further. The builders were doing their best to work around us, but that was going to be an even bigger problem when they started work on moving the staircase.

My second visit to the doctor didn't alleviate any of my concerns about the health of our baby, and the throbbing headache that our finances continued to give me, was not abating. Jesus, there was just so much to worry about: the baby, money, and trying not to make any more mistakes. I was so worried all the time. Of course, that meant I was distracted, very distracted. Here were our kids, our beautiful wonderful little kids, living in an open-ended Lego piece, being fed McDonalds and pizza, and in the company of a mad woman whose first reply to their every question, statement, or story was, "Hmm, what was that?"

Yet, I was trying. I was desperately trying to maintain normality, for all of us. I tried to make sure the kids did their regular stuff: homework, play-dates (disaster), swimming lessons, walks in the park, etc.

Added to that, I was doing my damnedest to maintain some level of attraction for my husband— this was a genuine uphill climb what with my rapidly expanding body, water retention in every limb, and hair that was all over the place, topped off with my newly thwarted, extension-induced mad, self-serving personality. And just as it couldn't get any worse, it did—along came the mice.

In all the time Niall and I have been together, no argument and no baby had ever induced a separate sleeping arrangement. All it took was a mouse. It was mid-October, during the early hours of a Saturday morning, and we were lying asleep in bed. I heard a scratch against the wall behind us, but I ignored it. Another scratch: a tad louder, a tad longer. I opened my eyes, looked over at Niall, and saw he was lying on his side with both arms and hands tucked under his pillow. Scratch, scratch, scratch. I lay very still, though I was quite awake by now. More scratching. *Christ!* I kept still, hoping that whatever it was might go away if I didn't move.

"I think we have some friends," was Niall's loud statement of fact.

I lost the plot. I leaped out of the bed and, with my pillow under my arm, and without a backward glance at Niall, I said, "I'm sorry Niall but I'm outta here."

I ran out of the room and into Adam's bedroom.

I slipped into his single bed beside Woody and the contraption that is Buzz Lightyear and, as I did so, his little voice said, "Mummy, I think I'll go back to my own bed now."

"Dote, you are in your own bed. Mummy just wanted to come into your bed instead, just for a change."

I didn't want to reveal to him then and there that this was actually going to be a permanent arrangement.

"Mmmm, it's hot mummy," he said but he was almost asleep again.

I didn't sleep a wink the entire night. The mice did me in. We had to move out. The house, now a bona fide building site, had gaps and draughts everywhere. The weather was turning cold, soon the stairs would be gone, and a ladder would be our only access upstairs. I was five months pregnant. I had to get real. Plus there were shagging mice in our house! Money or no money we could not stay any longer

7

The Travellers

We were moving to Cork, after all. We were going to stay with my parents for two weeks. Then we were moving to Blanchardstown in Dublin for another two weeks. A friend of mine lived in a townhouse in Clonee near Blanchardstown. She was going on a two week holiday to the Canaries at the beginning of November, and she offered us her home—for free! Blanchardstown is about 20 km from our house, but both locations are linked via the infamous M50, Dublin's ring road, which was just a two lane motorway at that stage. The location wasn't exactly ideal, and though it would mean crossing the city every morning and evening at peak times with three young children, at least I would get the boys to school, I would get to oversee the extension, and, most significantly, the accommodation was free, clean, and safe. *No complaints here!*

The joy that crossed Dave's face when I told him we were moving out was not lost on me. *Was I that bad?* Of course, he made all the right noises about it being the absolute correct decision, what with my condition, and the dangers posed to the kids. He sweetened it further by telling me that our moving out would accelerate the build and that things might well be finished ahead of time. I fell for that one too. I wanted to believe him. He asked that we bring whatever we'd need for the four weeks we would be out of the house. As Niall was travelling with work for the first two weeks, everything was loaded into my car and, for the foreseeable future, my car was going to be my constant base.

The car was packed with the precision of a boy scout—Niall is very proud of his lineage in that regard. Everything had its place, and he arranged it so that only the things I would need for Cork would be accessible, so I wouldn't have to unload the rest of the shebang until I left Cork. Easy knowing Niall had graduated as a scout leader too. My going to Cork for those two weeks really pleased him. He had to be abroad for this time, and he took great relief in knowing that his family would be well taken care of in Cork. And we were.

Those two weeks in Cork were precious. The kids enjoyed it, and I enjoyed it. Cleanliness had returned to our lives, and we once again consumed healthy fare. We missed Niall, but because everything was so clean, we soon got over it. This was probably the first time in my pregnancy that I had actually enjoyed being pregnant. I was still tired and still worried, but it was the first time I truthfully embraced my pregnancy, and didn't resent it. It was wonderful not to have to be talking beams, suspensions, and foundation depths, but rather baby names, babygros, and how the kids would get used to the new addition.

I loved having my Mum around, mothering me, feeding me, and taking over for me. Dad was great with the kids too and, with him around, they were never bored or cranky. Niall's parents, who only live 10 minutes from my own parents, took the kids to sweet shops, toyshops, and pound shops and refused them nothing. It was all so nice that I began to wonder whether we had been overhasty in our decision not to return to Cork in the first place.

Yet, our house in Dublin was never far from my mind, and I never let go of the controls. Despite Niall's insistence that I loosen the reins a little and give the builders some space, I continued to "oversee" things from Cork. I couldn't let it be and as the first week became the second, I began to find the distance frustrating. I needed to get back. By the end of the second week, I was ready to return, and I was happy to do so. The oasis of Cork was over.

Despite all Niall's great intentions with the arrangement of the car, it soon became undone in Cork. When I went to pack the car for our return journey, I didn't quite get the compact result he had initially achieved. There were duvets in the front seat, clothes overflowing from over-packed holdalls, toys in every crevice, and the seats yielded a harvest of discarded sweets.

The car was heaving for that return trip to Dublin. I inserted the "Sing-along Nursery Rhymes" cassette into the tape machine, and all the way back to Dublin we sang "Three Blind Mice", "Do you know the Muffin Man", and a feast of others. The kids loved this, and though I can never hear those songs and not think of this period in my life, they made for peaceful journeys and happy moments.

On our arrival back in Dublin, the plan had been to go straight to our new abode in Blanchardstown, where Niall was waiting for us, having returned from his travels. En route, however, my impatience to see the progress on the house got the better of me, so I made a detour. Instead of going north when I hit the M50, I headed south. The kids made this easy; they were asleep, exhausted by the prolonged stretching of their vocal cords. I didn't call Niall to tell him of the change of plan. He would have gone ballistic. With the kids still asleep in the car, I stood in front of our "home", and my heart sank. It didn't appear as though anything had been done in our absence. There was no way we would be in again in two weeks. What in God's name had they been doing?

I felt dizzy. I felt very dizzy. I called my brother Dermot who lived in Rathfarnham and asked him if I could drop by. I needed a cup of tea, fast, but I did not tell him I was feeling poorly; it would merely have prompted the now familiar refrain I was hearing from everybody: "Take it easy, Yvonne. Please take things easier." I was conscious of the fact that Niall was waiting on us in Blanchardstown, but I put off calling him because I did not want to have to explain my whereabouts. I hoped he would assume that I had had to make a few stops en route from Cork with the kids and was merely running a little behind.

Dermot, Frances, and their kids gave us a wonderful welcome, and my own kids, who were now very much awake, were thrilled at the unexpected treat of seeing their cousins. I, on the other hand, was feeling lousy. I sat with Frances and Dermot at their kitchen table while the kids played in another room. The room was cosy and warm and they made their evening meal stretch to include us. It was all so nice, until I suddenly fainted onto Dermot's shoulder. Even though Frances is the doctor, it was Dermot who took control. I can remember him carrying me up to their bedroom, laying me down, and pulling the sheets and blankets around me. He sat on the side of the bed and stayed with me, silent. This was a nice moment for me, but thoughts of Niall kept seeping through my consciousness. I needed to tell him where I was. I knew he would be worried.

"Where's my phone? I have to get up," I told Dermot.

"Yvonne, stay put; you are not going anywhere," Dermot insisted.

He was no match for me, and neither was Frances. The monster inside me emerged and, once again, I got my way. I hadn't seen Niall for a fortnight; I needed to see him. I needed to unpack that bloody car, and I needed to put down roots, even if it was for just two weeks. I lied to Dermot and Frances. I told them I was feeling much better, ushered my three protesting kids into the car, and began the drive to Blanchardstown. Stupid. But it was par for the course for the driven, single-minded, stubborn individual I had become, which in retrospect was terribly unfair to those around me, who all had their own concerns about me, and the baby.

My clothes were sticking to me, and I felt light-headed again. When I came down the slip road to the

M50, I remember saying to myself, "Now take it nice and slow, no rush, we just need to get there." It was dark but thankfully not busy. There was a large tow truck ahead with flashing sirens and I fell in behind it, following it at a snail's pace right across the M50 until the Blanchardstown exit—this somehow made me feel safe. My relief at reaching Blanchardstown without fainting, energised me so much that by the time Niall clapped questioning eyes on me, I wasn't quite the wreck of a woman I had been previously, and I made light of the stupid detour I had made. He let it go because it was just so good being together again.

8

The Floods

We were altogether again, in a little dolls house, a perfect house—a single, working girl's house. I was terrified. This was not a house for a heavily pregnant couple and their three children, all under the age of seven. I marvelled at my friend's generosity. Then I questioned her sanity. Then I canonised her. She was an angel who had given us her heaven for two weeks. Of course, I became impossible to live with. The kids were nagged to within an inch of their lives not to touch, spill, move, eat, or even play. If they had slept for the entire time that we lived there, that would have been fine by me. My only consolation was that we were out of the house for the most part of the day so there was some hope of maintaining a semblance of order in this pristine palace.

Niall left the house by 7.30 a.m. every morning with me and the kids leaving shortly afterwards. I had to have Adam in school by 8.50 a.m., and Luke had to be in playschool by 11.15 a.m. Laura stayed with me for the day. There was no point in returning to Blanchardstown in the interim, so I tended to live out of my car for the day. Laura, who was two at the time, and I project managed our build from there. It was miserable. But two very good supports came into play: Frances and Carmel. If it wasn't one of them, it was the other calling me as I crossed the M50 in the heavy morning traffic. "Can I take Laura today?" they would ask, and they always made it seem like I would be doing them a favour because their own kids needed company, and it was really about suiting themselves, not me at all. I was in the company of great kindness. This pattern of calls emerged casually every day, and it was a godsend. It afforded me the freedom to get things done, without an entourage. I was running to DIY shops, bathroom emporiums, window warehouses, and many other places besides. This kept me busy until I had to collect everybody at 3 p.m. and make the slow journey back to Blanchardstown, to the beat of our "Sing-along Nursery Rhymes" tape. This tape had not only become the soundtrack to all our travels, but the backing music to all my worries, on top of which another was added.

Our house was definitely not going to be ready by mid-November. With the end of our sojourn in Blanchardstown looming, we were left with no place to go. And we would have no place to go for quite some time. As regards timelines, the builders had a gift for evading my questions, helped by the fact that on most occasions they were up to their waists in mud induced by the consistent rainfall we were experiencing. Where were we going to live after the doll's house? Prior to arriving at a solution to that very question, an incident occurred that distracted us (as if a baby with an abnormal heartbeat, an extension that was going nowhere, and a daily commute of 20 km a day to school wasn't enough)—along came the floods.

The floods arrived one day in the first half of November, on a day probably forgettable enough for most people, but almost certainly remembered by anyone living in the west of the city at that time. On that day, the skies opened up and cried on the highways and byways of this country. We got caught right in the middle of it all.

When we had begun our build, we had also been given the green light to incorporate some land behind our garden wall, through which a small stream ran. There was a larger, higher wall behind the stream, and this would become our new boundary wall when we removed our original garden wall. Before this could happen, however, the stream had to be channelled and safeguarded, which involved it being encased in big circular concrete piping. The opportunity to acquire this additional land had also been open to three of our neighbours, and naturally we had all jumped at the opportunity. It was agreed that this work would coincide with our build, using our labourers for the task. Though this work was near completion on that day in November, it was not quite finished, and therein lay the crux of the impending disaster.

There had been warnings on the radio about this expected deluge of rainfall, and my intention was to get on the road back to Blanchardstown as early as possible. Niall had been in the UK, but having arrived back in the airport, he was now very close to our temporary home. The M50 had become a proverbial car park, however, and what should have taken him 30 minutes, cost him two hours.

Laura was in Frances and Dermot's house (again) and after collecting the boys from school, the rain was hammering off my windscreen as I swung by to collect her. En route, Niall phoned from the M50 and advised me to wait it out for a while as the motorway was a standstill in both directions. He told me that driving conditions were hazardous and he would prefer if I held off until the elements eased up. When I arrived at Frances's house, she had the same thoughts. She put dinner in the oven for us, put the kettle on, and directed me to sit by a roaring fire. The boys and Laura were delighted to stay and, once again, we availed of Frances's and Dermot's endless, swing-door hospitality.

The afternoon passed in a lovely way. Not since my stay in Cork, had I felt so relaxed. It was rare those days for me to wile away an afternoon drinking coffee, and chatting about nothing, with no urgencies, no pressures, and no deadlines. It was good too, to catch up in a real way with Frances because I was always running away from her, dropping Laura in the morning and collecting her in the afternoon. I felt good about having this time with her. The weather was of no importance, except that it afforded me a wonderful afternoon.

When Dermot arrived home at about 7 p.m., he told us the rain was easing and that we had probably seen the worst of it. I kept in touch with Niall, and at about 8 p.m., I felt I should head back to Blanchardstown. I called Niall to let him know we were on our way, and it was only after hanging up that I noticed the battery in my phone was low. I was relieved when we came down the slip road onto the M50 and saw there was no tailback and that, incredibly, traffic was flowing freely. It was raining again, but at least we were moving. The children were tired and cranky at this stage so I set "Let's Go Fly a Kite" to play, and peace reigned once more.

The rain started coming down hard, but I was moving fast. My phone rang and, thinking it was Niall, I turned down the nursery rhymes and reached for the phone. Without any salutation, I said, "We're doing great Niall, just great, no hold-ups at all."

But it wasn't Niall; it was *Kevin* my neighbour.

"Yvonne, it's *Kevin*," he said.

I thought, "Jesus, why does everyone call me?" but I said, "Hi *Kev*! Sorry, I was expecting Niall."

"Where are you?" he asked, and I was surprised at the question.

"Maybe you should come to the house. We have a real problem here, Yvonne," he continued. "The stream at the back of the houses has become a virtual river and has now overflowed. We are flooded right up to our back door!"

Oh fuck! The kids wanted the songs back on, and they also wanted my contribution because it had somehow become a prerequisite that I lead the chorus.

"Sing Mummy, sing!" they chanted from the backseat.

Shit, shit, shit!

"Jesus, *Kev*, I'm on the M50," I explained. *When am I not?*

The kids were like animals in a cage by now, and though I thought I had heard every conceivable sound I could from my children, the shrieks they emitted on that dark torrential evening surprised even me.

"*Kev*, I can't do anything tonight," I said, throwing some chocolate buttons (my last reserve of bribe food) to the pack of wolves in the back, buying me all of thirty seconds.

"Can you call Dave?" I asked.

Whether it was the mayhem in the background, the desperation of my own situation, or just the overall hopelessness of that night, he asked, "Are you okay?"

I was grateful.

"I'm grand *Kev*," I lied. "Grand."

When he finally hung up, I noticed my phone's battery was almost gone. *Shit!* World War III was now raging in the back seat of the car as Adam had devoured all the buttons, and the other two, feeling seriously hard done by, were wailing like banshees. I pressed play on the tape deck.

"I do like to be beside the seaside…" rang out. Everyone sang; harmony was restored. My phone rang again so the song was promptly turned off. It was Niall.

"Niall, we're just coming off the M50; my battery is nearly gone but we should be home soon," I said hurriedly.

"Mummy, turn back on the songs. Mummy, the songs!"

"I'm just talking to Daddy. I will now, just one sec guys," I entreated, but this only earned me more protests.

Niall ignored it all, and I thought, "Lovely if you can get away with it!" But then he spoke with an urgent tone.

"Yvonne, listen, the floods here are really bad. It was mad coming into the estate this evening. Now, I want you to listen to me carefully. When you come to the roundabout at the entrance to the estate, you have got to go up onto the footpath and drive between the wall and the lamppost. You will need to do the same at the other side of the roundabout. Do not go through the roundabout, it is too deep. Don't stall, keep your foot on the accelerator, and just concentrate on getting through it. Do you hear me, Yvonne? Can you hear me, Yvonne?"

Oh Jesus!

"What do you mean get up on the footpath?" I cried, and before I got my answer the phone went dead.

Fuck it! Fuck it! Fuck it!

"Mummy, sing, sing, sing!"

Oh Jesus.

I put the nursery rhymes back on and finally got some peace and quiet. I had plenty of time to get my head around things as I suddenly met the mother of all traffic jams.

"Pat a cake, Pat a cake, baker's man...." was beating out of the car radio, accompanied by three different versions in the back.

Oh God.

"Bake me a cake as fast as you can..." sang my very own choir of tenors, altos, and sopranos.

Oh Christ, will we ever get home?

"....and mark it with a B..."

I rested my head on the steering wheel. I just wanted to be home.

Wherever that is.

"Mummy, mummy, you're not singing!"

I raised and turned my head to look at my three little babies, singing their hearts out, smiling at me through the darkness. I smiled back at them, very weakly, and felt the strength draining from me.

"Sing Mummy!"

I started to mumble.

"Louder Mummy, can't hear you!"

I sang louder.

"Actions, Mummy!"

What else was I to do? I began the hand actions. *Well there's no driving to be done.* My actions were met with squeals of laughter. At least the kids were having fun. I really regretted telling Niall that we were nearly home. As the crow flies, we were about five minutes away but, in reality, we may as well have been a world away. I was really feeling his worry not to mention my own.

And this bloody roundabout! What in God's name was he going on about mounting pavements and stuff? That is if we ever get to this feckin' roundabout!

After a further 20 minutes, the tape was beginning to gnaw on my nerves, and my hand actions were flailing. The kids were getting restless, and wanted to do more than just move their arms. I turned off the tape. I couldn't deal with their hyperactivity on top of everything else. Amazingly, there were no more protests from the back.

First time ever!

I turned and looked at them again. These days, no two days were the same for them, what with all the upheaval, the travelling, and their demented mother. Recent life had been no picnic for these three little people. Then I remembered; it was Christmas. We were well into Phase I.

"Who wants to talk about Christmas?" I asked and Adam's hand flew up in the air.

"Okay, Adam, what are you most excited about?"

And suddenly, we were sorted. The conversation turned to all things Santa, and I let the questions flow as I knew they would. I was their sitting duck, their captive audience, and chief answerer of all their questions. It was the first occasion in a long time that I had engaged with them properly. The extent of my conversations with them of late had tended to revolve around manic bribes, broken promises, or desperate pleas. I had all the time in the world that evening, and as we crawled along the N3 towards Clonee amidst the lashing rain that dark November night, we had quite a thing going in that overloaded, overused, second home of a car. Listening to their happy banter, joining in with their awe at how Santa can conquer the world in just one night, I placed my hand on my tummy and felt like introducing myself all over again to this new little person within me because, let's face it, he couldn't have been altogether impressed with me thus far. An hour and a half after I had spoken with Niall, we finally hit the infamous roundabout.

Oh my God.

He hadn't exaggerated.

Oh my God.

There was an abandoned SUV stranded in the middle of the roundabout in very deep water. A smaller car was almost floating, and it too had been abandoned.

Oh sweet Jesus.

I could see what Niall had meant when he warned me not to attempt it. No one was. Every car ahead of me was mounting the footpath and navigating it at a snail's pace between the boundary walls and the lampposts. To get home I had to take the second exit, so I would have to ascend the pavement twice. I waited and watched as others went before me. I felt like an airplane on a runway, waiting to take off. Third in line, then second. My turn came. I did not hesitate. I kept my foot to the floor and lifted the car up onto the footpath.

Three kids in the back; three kids in the back! Keep cool! Keep cool!

I steered the car along the pavement, negotiating my obstacles beautifully. I had done it.

Oh, thanks be to God. Thanks be to God.

Now for the second ascent. No one else was going forward. Every car was taking the first exit. No one was continuing to mount a second time—did no one live in our section of this urban sprawl? Looking at it, the space between the lamp and the wall on the second leg of this challenge looked a whole lot narrower. Then I thought, maybe the cars in front knew something I didn't. Maybe the second exit had become more flooded since Niall had arrived two hours previously, so they were opting instead for the first exit. Maybe there was another way to get to our house. Maybe they all had updates on the situation—

my phone had been down for almost two hours, after all. I had received no recent brief. I didn't know what to do, but I decided to play it safe and took the first exit, following everyone else. I followed them through this patchwork of estates that overflowed across the plains. I did not know where I was going, but I was hoping that someone in front of me did.

The further I travelled, however, the more the cars in front and behind me fell away, until I was no longer part of a posse, but very much a lone traveller in the middle of an urban forest of "closes" and "crescents". There were flood waters everywhere. At one point, I had to mount a green to avoid a particularly big reservoir and was terrified that my wheels would jam in the sodden soil. I was beginning to lose all sense of direction and panic was welling up inside me. The children had fallen silent. I looked in the rear view mirror to see if they were sleeping. Their big black eyes stared back at me. They sensed I was lost, and it seemed their silence had come from an unspoken consensus to remain quiet so that Mummy could figure out how to get home. Mummy couldn't figure anything out.

I roamed aimlessly, drove into one cul-de-sac after another, each a replica of the one before. I had never before seen so many houses all packed into sequences of enclaves—home to so many people, but a no man's land to me. Spent, I pulled the car into the side of the road. The rain was beating down, and the glass had fogged up. I pressed the button to pull the window down, hoping to see a street sign. I could see nothing. It was 11 p.m. at this stage. I looked at the house which I had stopped in front of. The lights were on, and there appeared to be movement in the front room. I turned to Adam.

"I am just going to run into the house here honey and ask the people inside if I can call Daddy. It's just that my battery is down," I said, trying to sound like everything was perfectly normal. He nodded, but his eyes were wide with fear. Tiredness was etched on his little face, and his normally olive toned skin had taken on a white pallor.

"I won't go in; you will see me the whole time," I assured him.

Again he nodded. I opened the car door and made a run through the downpours to the front porch. I rang the doorbell. Thankfully, they opened the door to me, but they were understandably wary.

"I am lost," I explained. "I have three kids in the car, and my phone is dead. Can I please make a call to my husband?"

They were young, maybe in their early-twenties. They didn't appear in the least bit concerned about my predicament. Nor did they offer me any invitations to come inside. But they handed me their phone, for which I was very grateful. I stood in their porch, my eyes never leaving the car, and I called Niall. He answered immediately. His anxiety was palpable.

"Where are you Yvonne? Where in God's name are you?" There was no accusation in his voice, no impatience—just desperation.

I started to cry.

"Ssssh," he soothed. "Just tell me where you are."

"I haven't a notion, not a notion, Niall. All I know is that I am parked outside a house in front of a green." It never even dawned on me to ask my reluctant hosts inside where I was, and it didn't appear to strike Niall either.

"Will you come and get us? Will you just come and get us?" I asked him.

"I'll find you; I'll find you. Just stay put!" he instructed me.

I left the phone on the floor of the hall, and shouted a thank you to the people inside the house, through their closed living room door. I shut the front door behind me and ran back to the car. Only then did I notice that I hadn't pulled the driver's window back up. My seat was drenched.

"Oh my God, guys, are ye soaked?" I asked of the three white faces.

There was no answer, just three pairs of shining eyes blinking back at me. I went to press the button to pull the window back up, but it was a no go. I tried again and again. Nothing. I got back out of the car and tried to wedge it up with my two hands. Useless. I was soaked through. We sat there, just the four of us, with the rain pouring in the window, in this unfamiliar concrete jungle, in a part of the city that was far from home, and we waited for Niall to come. He didn't arrive in a Superman outfit, but when I saw him emerge from the darkness, striding purposely towards us, defiant in the rain, I felt the burden of this endless night slip from my shoulders, and I was very much his Lois Lane.

9

Townsend Street

We were moving again—this time to Townsend Street in Dublin's inner city, to one of those new, gated, "exclusive" apartment blocks that were springing up all over the city. My other brother Declan and his wife, Regina, offered it to us, for free! Their tenants had moved out and rather than let it again, they gave it to us, indefinitely, for as long as it took to finish our house. It was an answer to our prayers. I found it uncanny how people always seemed to read our minds because we never openly discussed our woes. The emerging crease lines on our foreheads and around our eyes must have told a thousand stories.

Moving back home was still a long way off. We gave our immediate attention to the problem of the stream (leaving our house "workerless" for a week), but thankfully our neighbours' angers subsided along with the flood waters. We may not have had a house, but at least we were still friendly with the neighbours.

Townsend Street, much like Blanchardstown, wasn't the most ideal location. As the crow flies, it was much nearer to home, but the traffic every morning and evening was once again dictating our arrival and departure times. The apartment itself was a haven at the core of Dublin city, but it was sparsely furnished with a bed in each room and a set of a table and chairs. That was it. The tenants had had their own furniture that, naturally, they had taken with them when they left and, as there was no time to furnish it before our invasion, we were just very grateful to have a roof over our heads.

We borrowed a portable TV and took a mattress from home to act as our temporary couch. We packed it into my car and made our way to our new base in town. The kids loved the place. For one, I wasn't quite the same maniac I had been in Blanchardstown. Two, they were allowed to eat, drink, and jump on the "couch". Three, they loved when we all cuddled up together to watch TV on the mattress, even though they couldn't get their heads around the "baby TV" or the fact that we only had four channels, two of which were fuzzy. Four, they loved to see Niall pull me out of the mattress every time I needed to get up, which turned out to be quite often because pressure on certain organs made for frequent trips to the loo. Five, they loved the balcony, onto which they were never allowed venture (I was still a bit of a maniac in that department) and, finally, the cherry on top, they adored the elevator. I quite liked the elevator myself as my size was no longer conducive to negotiating stairwells. Plus, I was suffering from severe sciatica, and I never knew when to expect those sporadic darts of pain that were making this pregnancy most uncomfortable.

I would look at myself in the mirror (for all the sparseness of furnishings in the apartment, there was a full length mirror in the en-suite) after emerging from the shower. I couldn't very well have missed myself. I remember seeing a stranger looking back at me. Well not quite a stranger, but a woman I had known a long time ago who, with the passage of time, had really let herself go, and wasn't easily recognisable. My youth seemed to have deserted me. Everything was an effort. I had lost the drive for the build; I truly didn't give a damn anymore. I just wanted to be a proper family again, in a proper home, with proper priorities.

The greatest comfort I had, however, was that the baby was kicking. Good, strong, hard kicks. At times when I was lying in bed, Niall and I would gaze at the extraordinary movements of my belly, an entity all of its own. Sometimes, I felt we could have shaken hands with our baby's foot. We would giggle and laugh, talk to the baby, ask him to ease up because we were "getting enough kicks out here", but mostly we were just relieved. It was good that he was this strong; he was a fighter. Even though his little heartbeat was still not tapping right, all this Kung Fu action made it easier for us to believe the doctor was right when he explained that the heartbeat anomaly was merely a characteristic of this particular pregnancy.

The journey from Townsend Street to school in Ballinteer every morning was not quite as onerous as the one from Blanchardstown, and although traffic was heavy, the distance was a fraction of what it had been, so it was altogether a much easier process. The new school run brought me past the front door of Holles Street Hospital every morning and, without fail, each time I passed it, a knot of excitement would form in my belly. I loved Holles Street. I would have had babies just to spend time there. When there, my only task was feeding and changing my new baby, and my only decision was what to eat for breakfast, dinner, and tea.

I remember my first experience of Holles Street as a first time mother. God, I was naive. First and foremost, I had gone 18 days over my due date, and I was virtually on the cusp of climbing Mount Everest in order to shift the baby. When I was 10 days over my due date, my doctor asked that I visit him every second day, just so he could check the fluid surrounding the baby. It was fine, until day 18, a Tuesday in late June, 1995, the hottest summer ever. The doctor told me it was time; I was to be induced. I nearly died. I wasn't ready. I was terrified. Niall, on the other hand, was elated. He had my bag packed for the last four weeks (there goes my boy scout again), and his moment had arrived. *Thunderbirds are go!*

"Now," Niall told me. "You'll need a good feed, so we'll stop off at the Frog Diner in Baggot Street. You'll need it, Yvonne, to keep you going."

I was in a daze, so I went along with whatever he told me, though I was finding his enthusiasm a tad patronising. When an enormous plate of fries, a cheeseburger, and a banana malt appeared in front of me, I nearly threw up.

"Niall, I'm sick," I told him. "I can't do this," I said, meaning deliver the baby not eat the food, though I couldn't do that either. "They say the pains are much harder when the baby's induced." He put his hand through the malt tankards to grab mine and squeezed it.

"We'll get through it, Yvonne," he said. "We will get through this." He paused for a moment before asking, "Will I eat your chips so?"

I wanted to be him. He got to have the same as me, a baby, but he didn't have to do any of what I had to do. We were still living in Rathmines, and we returned there to collect all that we had prepared for this momentous day. Just as we were leaving the bedroom, I asked, "Niall, can we just kneel down and say a prayer… that I'll get through this?" *Forget this "we" business.*

So we knelt in our bedroom and said a prayer, and just as I was blessing myself, I got my very first contraction. I had gone into labour. This delighted Niall even further because he finally got to do the whole racing to the hospital thing, blowing any vehicle or pedestrian within a 10 m radius out of our path. I wouldn't have minded, but my contractions were about 15 minutes apart; I had plenty of time. However, his crescendo came when he threw the car right outside the front door of Holles Street. Mission completed. He had to retrieve it later.

He had gotten his moment; next up, was mine.

I was brought up to the delivery suites where another woman was making some rather unpleasant noises. They had told us during our ante-natal classes that we might have to share a room while in labour, but we would deliver in private. We waited in this room for about 20 minutes, and though my contractions were getting stronger, I was not too uncomfortable. The same could not be said of the poor lady next to us. She was gasping and moaning; her discomfort was terribly disconcerting. Shortly afterwards, she was wheeled out of our room, and Niall and I were left alone. I panicked. I looked to Niall and then sought out the nurse. When I found her I asked her a question that can only be asked by a woman who has not given birth before.

"Are we about to have our baby, now?"

The nurse just looked at me and resisted what must have been an enormous urge to slap me. As dry as you like, she answered, "No sweetheart, she is."

Eight hours later I knew all about it.

That all seemed like such a long time ago that Christmas in 2002. There we were: two more babies added to our brood and, very soon, there would be another little face in the back seat, another little personality to get to know, another little person to love. *Loved already.*

Though life in Townsend Street was working out reasonably well, we were beginning to get anxious about when we could return home for good. I was prepared to do anything to expedite this, and there came a day when I was compromised in this regard. I arrived at the house to find the whole backside of it opened up to the four winds, and the builders up to their shoulders in grime, trying to fit a whole wall of windows that we had not ordered.

There were four of them, each one admirably focussed on the job in hand. Four muddy men. The rain was coming down in sheets, and it seemed the wind was shaking the very ground beneath my feet. Despite the elements, the men were perspiring and tense, but the only thing that mattered to my eyes was the fact that the windows were the "wrong fucking windows".

I hesitated.

Oh, does it matter? Does it really matter? I want to come home. Just run with it, Yvonne; leave it and run with it!

I couldn't; I just couldn't. There was some drive in the old girl yet.

"Lads, these are not the windows we ordered," I said, in much the same way that Niall had told me we had mice. Not a nice fact but, nonetheless, it had to be said. They paused. Then looked at each other.

"What do you mean?" one of them asked.

"These are not the windows we ordered," I repeated. *Is there an alternative interpretation of this statement?*

A look passed between all of them. They were clearly pissed off.

"But sure aren't they grand," one of them asked, reminding me of the bank clerk.

"Sure they are grand," I answered, and for the third time, I repeated, "but they are not the windows we ordered."

One of them decided to take control. *Where on earth is Dave?*

"Okay love, so let's say we get the ones you ordered, but to do that you know you won't be in for Christmas?"

This was either a threat or a bluff. Either way, I said for the fourth time, "These are not the windows we ordered."

The next day the correct windows arrived and were fitted. *Phew!*

These situations really weren't good for any of us. Relations were tense, conversations strained, and requests became demands yet, ironically, we all wanted the same thing (albeit in different directions) —the builders wanted out, and we wanted in, before Christmas. We were now well into December, and it never seemed to be daytime. Our journey to school every morning was in darkness, and our return journey home was also in darkness. The children had become very patient travellers, and though the songs still played their part, we had introduced a couple of new games to wile away our hours spent in traffic—"Counting Christmas Trees" and "Counting Cranes".

The world outside the windows of my car in December 2002 made for interesting viewing and kept my children enthralled. The Dublin landscape boasted of the times we were living through. It was a pretty vista to see the dozens and dozens of cranes that marked the Dublin skyline, all lit up in sequences of fairy lights—a host of new stars that twinkled just for Christmas. Big and tastefully decorated Christmas trees stood in the bay windows of the grand old Georgian houses on Palmerstown Road, the fun and silliness of office parties spilled out of the crowded pubs and restaurants of Ranelagh, and as we journeyed onto the flatlands of Pearse Street and Townsend Street, candle pyramids dotted every window of the old tenement blocks. Jesus would have had his choice of accommodation down in Townsend Street that Christmas. The morning of 12 December dawned on our last day in Townsend Street. We were going home.

Home was still in a state of mayhem, but it was a mayhem we could handle. We had been out of our house for seven weeks. We were going home. Everything was getting back to normal.

10

A Broken Heart

Thursday, 17 December 2002 brought an end to any ambitions we had of getting back to normal. Our baby had a hole in its heart. That evening, I left the "bad news" room and Holles Street behind. I walked up the side of Merrion Square, towards the ESB Headquarters which my car was parked in front of. I sat in the car and looked out onto the busy street. It was after 7 p.m., and it was teaming with revellers, workers, commuters, and lovers. I was dry-eyed, but numb. It was like I was no longer a part of the world; I was just looking in on it. I thought over the past year: the planning, the excitement, the irritations, and the struggles. I thought about my controlling, my immersion, the commuting, and the travelling. I saw the faces of those around me, my husband, my parents, my family, and my friends—pleading, concerned, and anxious. I saw it all clearly. It was too late.

I have broken my baby's heart.

I called my mother, and I started to cry.

I have broken my baby's heart.

My journey home that evening, Niall's arrival home that night, collecting the kids, my breaking the news to Niall —it's all a blur, a memory I cannot rightly recall. The only picture I have of that evening is of Niall and I sitting in a kitchen that had not yet boiled an egg, at a table that had not yet served a meal, in a room that echoed our voices. What was ahead for us? What was ahead for our children? What was ahead for our baby? We just had to wait to find out. We had to wait for the next scan, only this time in Crumlin Children's Hospital. I had never been there before. We were seeing a specialist. Someone who would make it all go away. It was scheduled for four days time, the Monday before Christmas. We had the whole weekend to go, a whole weekend of waiting. Then Frances called.

"I got the appointment moved up," she told us. "It'll be Saturday; Saturday morning, 10.30 a.m." *In the company of kindness.*

"Can you come with us?" I asked her.

Without hesitation, she replied, "I can."

We needed a translator. We needed a witness. We needed someone outside of us, but who was still a part of us, to tell us that this was really happening. We needed to know what we should and should not expect, and I really needed to know what to pray for. The next day, Friday, I collected Adam from school. After all the recent upheaval, I was so anxious that, as far as the kids were concerned, life would return to normal. He ran ahead of me and was seated and waiting for me as I caught up to him. I leaned in to fasten his seatbelt and heard a movement behind me. It was a mother from the school.

"Hi, Yvonne," she said.

I turned around and took my head out of the car.

"Hi there," I replied. I couldn't quite think of her name.

"I just want to say I am so sorry to hear about your baby," she said, her face downcast.

What? How does she know about it? And why is she sorry? My baby's not dead!

I mumbled something, got into the car, and drove off.

"What's wrong with the baby, Mummy?" I heard Adam asking from behind.

"What love? What's that?" I said, reverting to my old reliable sound pieces to buy me some time.

"*Megan's* Mum, she said she was sorry about the baby; why is she sorry about the baby, Mummy?"

I cursed *Megan's* Mum. I thought quickly. *What do I say, what do I say?* Niall and I hadn't gotten to this part yet. We hadn't fully grasped the reality of things ourselves, let alone thought about telling the children. It hadn't even been 24 hours since we'd heard the news. *How did she know?*

"The baby is fine, sweetheart, just fine," I said. "However, there is just a small little problem that the doctors need to fix, and tomorrow Daddy and I will be going to see the doctor who will fix the baby."

"Mmm, well that's okay then. You know *James* was really mean to *Fiona* in school today, he…" and he was off. *Thank God.*

What I had just said was right; bang on, in fact. Our baby was fine. Just fine. Plenty of babies were born sick, plenty, and they all got better. *That's going to be our Crumlin experience.* That was my thinking and outlook as we travelled to the hospital the following morning. I was upbeat and ready for whatever the day would bring. We were a strong unit, Niall and I. We would survive this, and so would our baby.

We were shown to the specialist's room, where the three of us took a seat in a waiting room that was more like a hallway. I sat there, the hospital in my nose, wondering if this was something I would ever get used to. Would this environment ever become familiar to me? Would I, at some time in the future, know the names of the nurses passing me by today?

Up until then, this was a parallel universe whose existence was immaterial to mine. Now suddenly, I was in its very bosom, dependent and scared. The doctor arrived. He was young, early forties, handsome, and dressed casually, but stylishly. In tow behind him was his young son of perhaps 10 or 11. Frances stood up to greet him, and they talked in hushed tones. It was only then that I realised how Frances' contacts had pulled this meeting off. I turned my gaze to the little boy, and I saw it was he who had paid the price that day; a delay in the midst of his special day with Daddy, planned long before the likes of Niall and I had come crashing in on top of it.

The doctor turned to us and asked that we continue on into another room. He bent down to his son, passed him something, and patted him on the shoulder before following us into the surgery. Once again, I was asked to settle myself on the bed. Niall and Frances sat to the left of me, while the doctor sat to my right bedside the monitor. He positioned it in such a way that we could all see it. The scan began.

The whole procedure lasted over an hour. *A long time to keep a child waiting.* Again, the movement of the sonogram on my tummy was irritating and tiring. The monitor told me nothing. I looked to Niall's face to chart the evolvement of events. He was completely absorbed by what he saw, though he was absently rubbing his thumb over the back of my hand. That was irritating me too. As the process progressed, I was shocked by an overwhelming desire to sleep. I just felt so very tired. For a long time, there was no conversation. There was no guided tour to what we were seeing. It was just us witnessing him do his work—assessing the problem so he could determine his plan of action.

He eventually turned to Frances and started highlighting different features, using terminology that revealed nothing to me. Niall, however, was hooked on his every word. Niall was lucky in that regard. This whole environment was the backdrop to his job. None of this intimidated him, alienated him, or threatened him. Indeed, he was on a first name basis with some of the people we had met on the way in here. He didn't need a spell in hospital with a sick child to get to know everyone. I, on the other hand, was just waiting until someone was ready to speak to me in plain English. Finally, the specialist turned off the monitor and leaned back in his chair, causing it to move back a little on its wheels. He was ready to talk to us.

He began to describe the heart as having four vessels and chambers, and he outlined the function of each one of them. I was transported back to my second year biology class. He drew us a diagram of how our baby's heart was presenting. It was a peculiar picture, unsightly in its deviance from what a normal heart should look like: baby's heart versus normal heart. I thought of the doctor, all those years ago, slapping the charts with his ruler. *How are we going to get from here to there?*

After some further biology speak, the specialist turned to me and said, "The best way I can describe this to you is to say there has been a complete malformation of the baby's heart."

"You mean the hole?" I clarified. I was determined to have my say.

He paused, glanced at Frances, leaned towards me, his chair gliding closer, and very gently explained, "This isn't so much about a hole in the baby's heart, Yvonne; this is about the heart itself not progressing. It is about the heart mal-forming."

There was a moment of complete silence.

"Mal", the French word for bad—that's ironic! The prettiest language telling me the ugliest news...

Niall was the first to break the silence: "So... what? The heart is what? No good? Not functional? Is it functioning now? What?" he asked.

I looked at Niall; it was the first time I had seen him lost.

"The heart does not need to function inside the womb; Yvonne's heart is doing the work for the baby. However, the problem will arise upon its birth. As it stands, the baby will not survive without intervention."

It was my turn to speak: "Well we knew that, isn't that why the baby needs to be taken here to Crumlin at birth, for intervention, emergency surgery, right?" *We know this already.*

"This scan has revealed many more complications than originally viewed in Holles Street. Initially, we didn't know the extent of the damage."

Damage? Oh God, what did I do?

The doctor continued, "We have a better idea now. Now we see that it is not only the heart itself but..." he paused to glance at Frances, then back to us, before continuing, "the arteries, the main arteries going to and from the heart, appear to be deformed, mangled, if you will. The extent of which, again, we will not know until birth." He paused again before telling us, "I'm sorry."

Sorry? Again, someone's sorry. My baby is not dead!

Silence filled the room once more, and after several moments it was once again broken by Niall: "What kind of life can we expect for our child?" he asked.

Child? Niall has already zoomed ahead to teaching him to ride a bike.

"The quality of your baby's life is compromised," the doctor answered. "Should the problems presented at birth be operable and successful, the best we could hope for in a situation like this would be a life expectancy of up to early adulthood."

What? No! This can't be happening. The best we could hope for?

As if in answer to my thoughts, the doctor spoke again: "I need to advise you that this would be the best outcome and, even at this, it would be a long road for you and your child. There would be many major operations, particularly in the baby's formative years, and a life restricted from all the normal expectations, possibly confined to a wheelchair for much of the time due to any potential strains on the heart."

No bike riding then.

"However, I must underline that I cannot gauge the full extent of the challenge until birth."

Oh dear God. Dear Mary, Mother of God. Sweet Jesus, this cannot be happening.

"I need to say something else here," the doctor persisted, and I wondered what else he could possibly have to say. "If I feel I cannot prolong life beyond a year, I will not operate on your baby," he said matter-of-factly. After a brief pause he added more gently, "I would be giving you false hope to do so, and it would be a year of heartbreak for you, your children, and your baby."

A broken heart; all our broken hearts. I said nothing. After a moment, Niall spoke again, and I wondered how he was still capable of speaking.

"So we just have to hope that the heart isn't quite as deformed as you might fear?" he asked, giving me my prayer.

"Let's hope not," the doctor responded softly. Then, suddenly, he asked, as normal as can be, "Do you know the sex? Do you want to know the sex of the baby?"

I was on autopilot now. "No, No. We don't. We want it to be a surprise," I told him. Whoever it was that said there were few surprises in life must have been very lucky.

Frances thanked the doctor and exchanged greetings for Christmas. As she did so, for the first time in all my pregnancies, Niall took over the job of cleaning the gel from my bump. He did it slowly and with care, and it seemed to me that it was not me he was cleaning and tendering to, but the baby—the only thing he could do for his child in this useless situation.

On the way out, we passed the little boy who was now running towards his Daddy. His father's work was done; his special day had begun.

Happy Christmas.

We travelled home through the Christmas traffic, past packed shopping centres, decorated pubs, and festive homes. We let ourselves into our new house, still a stranger to us. All was quiet. The kids had been outsourced, and they had yet to be fetched. We walked into the living room, not quite knowing what to do with ourselves. There in front of us stood three new couches, delivered while we were out. There were two wine coloured couches and one white one—results of decisions made a lifetime ago when that kind of thing had rocked my world. We both sat down, silently, on one of the wine couches. We said nothing, but both of us were looking in the same direction—at the white couch. We sat there for some time, lost in our own thoughts. Then Niall spoke: "That is the most beautiful couch I have ever seen… but it is by far the most stupid thing we have ever done." I nodded in agreement. *What does it matter now?*

11

Christmastime

That weekend and over the following days, people dropped into us with presents, chocolates, bottles of wine, and a variation of sorry looks. They all admired the house, and everyone was grateful for the distraction it afforded because it meant that none of us had to talk about the baby. *Lovely house; shame about the baby.* I hadn't been Christmas shopping at all. What with living out of a car for the past few months, building a new house, and getting serious diagnoses of babies, I had just never gotten to the shops. So on the Monday before Christmas, when Niall came home from work, I told him I wanted to go shopping. I needed to get out into the crowds, be ordinary, do ordinary things, and get excited about silly stupid things—I just needed to get out, and I wanted to get out alone. I felt trapped. It was a bad idea.

I walked through the mall like a woman on a mission. I was searching for families, families like us, families like the "us" we used to be. When I found them, my envy was like a knife. Why could we not go back there? Why could we not be ordinary again? Why, oh why, had we gone for a fourth child? *Hadn't we got things pretty near perfect already? Why didn't we just leave well enough alone?* That night walking around that shopping centre, I fell into a sort of mental abyss. I am not sure if it had to do with anger, anger at ourselves for pushing the boundaries, or if it had more to do with regret, regret at not quitting while we were ahead. I was sure of one thing, however; I had a fear—a fear that was overwhelming me. My fear was twofold: one that our baby would die, and two: a confusing, disturbing and guilty fear—that our baby would live, and our lives would never be the same again.

I came home that night, my ankles swollen and sore from the miles of polished floors I'd conquered. My sciatica had kicked in, and I was walking with a limp. The baby lay heavily on my pelvis, and I put my hand under the bump in an effort to lighten it. I was cold and tired, and I felt ugly inside and out. As I pulled into the driveway, I saw that Niall had the fire on, he had fixed the Christmas tree lights, and the house was a beacon of Christmas cheer. While I was out, he had made our new house a home. I parked my car in the driveway, and I looked at all before me. I had a lovely home to walk into, a wonderful man to wrap me up, and three beautiful, happy children to cuddle. My guilty fear grew.

12

"If I was your wife...?"

Christmas came and went. New Year was quiet. The real countdown for us was in February. The doctors had advised me to receive a weekly scan until birth. They were not going to intervene unless circumstances dictated there was a need to and, all going well, I would carry our baby to full term and could expect a normal delivery. So it was that on Thursday, 9th January 2003, a wet and dark afternoon, and the day after Christmas formally closed, I drove to Holles Street, alone. I had persuaded Niall to stay in work. This expedition to Holles Street was going to be a weekly ritual for the next seven weeks, and he needed to save his favours and holidays for a period when we would really need them.

Once again I found myself in the waiting room. I was not nervous, and the wait was short before they called me in. I decided I was going to be more assertive this time, take more control. It was the first time I had seen my doctor since the scan in Crumlin.

Once I was on the bed, and before he commenced with the now familiar process, I asked him a direct question: "If I was your wife, how would you feel about all this?"

He hesitated for a moment, but only to place himself in the hypothetical situation. "I would be concerned," he answered truthfully. "I would not be happy, but I would still be hopeful."

I bet he's glad he's not married to me.

I lay back and let the scanning procedure take over again. I thought I might have gotten it right with the clothes this time—for once. I wasn't in the least bit self-conscious, and I even managed to facilitate him in getting full access to the bump! I wondered, however, whether this had more to do with the fact that I really didn't give a damn anymore. For the first part of the scan, I just looked up at the ceiling, concentrating on moulds in the plasterwork and odd stains here and there. I wondered absently how they got there and how they could be removed. The scan was going on a bit though.

I took my eyes away from the ceiling and looked at my doctor's face. He was looking serious. *What now?* As the foetal expert, he was scanning this baby with a practised expertise. I looked from his face to the monitor. His focus was not the heart. He appeared to be taking measurements of the head, hands, and feet. Then it seemed he was zooming in on the baby's face. *Oh Jesus.* I knew what he was doing. He was looking for other abnormalities, other complications and potential syndromes. *Oh, how stupid am I?* After Crumlin, I really thought things could not get any worse, but lying there knowing my doctor was checking for every conceivable abnormality, gripped me and numbed me. My whole body became a dead weight. I held my breath for a long time. Then he suddenly stopped. He wrapped up the sonogram and replaced it in its hold. Then he sat back and looked at me straight.

Here it comes.

I was still lying down with my bump exposed, and the excesses of the scan gel were rolling down my sides.

"Yvonne, I'm going to answer your question again. If you were my wife, you would be back in here tomorrow morning to have the baby delivered."

I couldn't believe it. I very nearly said, "But I'm not your wife, so…" as if that would have dictated a different manner of treatment. "Are you serious?" I asked instead.

"I am Yvonne," he said. "We need to take the baby out; you will need to undergo a Caesarean Section in the morning."

"What about the natural course of things?" I reminded him. "I thought it would be better to deliver close to my time and to deliver naturally; what about all that?"

I always go overdue; you know that—why not this time?

"It needs to happen now, Yvonne," he said as if reading my thoughts, and then gently he said, "We need to go in."

Suspicion crept into my mind.

"You found something else wrong with the baby, didn't you?" I accused him.

"Yvonne, I did a full examination on the baby, which is procedure in these instances. From my examination I have found nothing else; the problems and complications rest with the heart and the arteries."

"Does my baby have Downs Syndrome?" I asked him, still disbelieving. I asked him about the only real syndrome I knew anything about, and I didn't even know a whole lot about that. "Downs Syndrome babies usually have heart problems, don't they?" I asked, full of my own importance.

"They can do," he answered calmly, "but not of this nature. I don't believe your baby has Downs Syndrome."

I didn't know how to feel about that. I wasn't sure if I was relieved or disappointed. *Don't Downs Syndrome kids get to live normal lives?* But no, my baby didn't have that kind of heart problem. *What in God's name do I know about anything?* Now I was yearning to have a Downs Syndrome child! I wasn't recognising my own feelings, my own reactions. I was trying to put down yardsticks in a muddy field, and I kept slipping.

I don't belong here. None of this fits. Let's just go back to the original plan: I am expecting a baby, I deliver a baby, and we all go home together. Please, none of this other stuff.

I made my return to the bad news room where I was left to make my calls. Everything was the same: the walls, the clock, the loveseat, and the box of tissues. It was all redundant to me, particularly the tissues. I didn't need them because tomorrow was going to be a happy day; tomorrow I would be having a baby.

I left the bad news room and made the now familiar walk from Holles Street up by Merrion Square to where my car was parked, and I began my journey home. On the way, I stopped off in a local pharmacy to buy a new vanity bag. I took my time looking around, and the assistant was helpful and made friendly enquiries. I told her with a smile that I was going into hospital in the morning to have my baby, and we both looked at my bump. She got all excited, and so did I. We chose the vanity case together. It was a good choice, and she threw me in a few free samples of moisturisers. As she totted up my bill on the register, she asked me if I knew the sex. I told her I didn't, but she asked me if I had an idea. I told her I did. Then she said, assuredly, that it didn't really matter though did it? I agreed and told her it didn't. She continued, and shared her firm opinion with me that all that mattered was that it was a healthy baby. I told her she was absolutely right.

Though I was seven weeks ahead of time, my boy scout didn't let me down. He had had my bag packed for a month already. Thankfully, we didn't need to rush off to buy babygros for the baby. We had bought them earlier in the pregnancy. They say it's bad luck to do that.

We organised for my older brother Declan to collect the kids at 7.30 a.m. the following morning. That night I went up to the bedroom. My mother-in-law had bought me a pair of lovely satin pink pyjamas for Christmas—I would wear that for our first photo together. I painted my fingernails and my toe nails, an acrobatic feat. I looked at my legs and decided they needed to be de-haired. I asked Niall if hair removal cream would damage the baby, but he thought not. I applied the hair removal cream, left it on too long, and couldn't sleep all night because my legs were tingling.

We got up at 6.30 a.m. I was relieved not to have to try to sleep anymore. We woke the children and got them dressed. My little Laura asked me if we were going to have the baby today. I told her we were, and she said, delightedly, that she was going to be a big sister. I told her she was. She asked why she couldn't come with me, and I told her it would be boring, and that her cousins would be disappointed if she didn't go see them. She agreed. Declan arrived early and held me close before he took the three children away in his car. We were alone in the house again. *"Lovely house; shame about the baby."*

We got into the car and were in no mad rush. No honking the horn, no crashing red lights; we had plenty of time. There was very little traffic, and we found a convenient car space. Niall put money in the meter. It was all very calm. We crossed the road to Holles Street to have our baby.

13

A "blue" baby

Everyone kept telling us that our baby would be "blue". Our own doctor had told us this, the specialist in Crumlin had warned us of this, and every medical worker we met the day of our baby's birthday made sure we were aware of this. We got it. We were having a "blue" baby.

To cater for our "blue" baby, we had come up with a plan. Simple really, Niall was to stay with the baby at all times. My parents were travelling up from Cork, and they would sit with me. At about 10 a.m., a nurse came into our cubicle. She had one of those faces that didn't invite you to contradict her. She drew the curtain around the bed and asked Niall to move to the other side. She explained that she had to prepare me for surgery and, with me nodding compliantly, she opened my gown and started to shave my pubic hair—terrific, a Brazilian in Holles Street. She then got out some cotton balls, poured some sort of disinfectant liquid onto them, and started to remove my carefully applied nail polish. Though I had accepted the Brazilian without question, I asked about the nail varnish. She told me they needed to see the colour beneath my nails during surgery. To think, I could have saved myself all those acrobatics! She put a shower cap on my head and told me the doctor would be with me shortly. Then, abruptly, she left.

I looked at Niall. I felt very unattractive, but he looked at me as if I was the most beautiful girl in the world. A female doctor who I hadn't met before came in. She was assertive, and keen for us to appreciate the gravity of our situation. This she did by summing up all that we already knew. We nodded at each familiar detail and statement of fact. Once again our "blue baby" was referred to, and she explained the reasons for this. We were told our baby's heart was incapable of pumping all the blood to his lungs, so his blood was not being fully oxygenated and, therefore, he would be blue. She put down the chart she had been holding like a charter and paused. Resuming in the same matter-of-fact manner, she calmly told us that there was every chance our baby would die today.

With that, I was wheeled into the operating room. I had never been operated on before, and the environment reminded me of the cookery room in my primary school. The smells were different, naturally, and everyone wore a mask. Coincidentally, the room was very blue. Niall was with me when they gave me the epidural. I had only had that once before, on Adam, and I was terrified of it. Once they administered it, they asked Niall to leave while they prepared me for the birth.

Oh please don't leave, please.

He must have seen the terror in my eyes and asked if he could stay. They gently, but firmly, refused and assured him he would be returned for the birth. I was alone. Once again, I was on a hospital bed staring at a ceiling. There were no bumps in the plasterwork here, no old stains. It was all lights, pendulums, and glare.

I switched my gaze to the anaesthetist, a lady with lovely eyes. She appeared to be in control, a firm woman. In Niall's absence, she became my focus. As she went about her business, issuing instructions and handing out orders, she maintained a conversation with me. She talked to me with an optimism that I was beginning to feel was a rarity in Holles Street, commending me on going for a fourth child. She treated me as a regular patient, not a walking time bomb of gloom. Though she must have known my history, I liked to think she didn't. She made me feel normal. *An extraordinary thing to be normal in pregnancy...* Then Niall appeared. *Lovely, lovely Niall.* I shifted my gaze to my husband's familiar shiny eyes. I felt safe again.

Then, suddenly, I was gasping, I couldn't breathe. I needed air. *Someone please give me air.* Niall was asking me questions, but I couldn't answer, I couldn't breathe. I couldn't speak. *I am going to die of suffocation.* Then I was retching. Someone held a sick bowl in front of me, but nothing came up. My insides were being pushed and stretched and pulled. It was like someone was rearranging all my internal organs. I could feel their hands on my innards. *Oh dear God, I am seriously going to die of suffocation.*

Then, the most wonderful vision emerged, diminishing all else. He was held high for us to see: our son, long, lean, and perfectly formed. He was kicking and punching the air. I heard him cry. Then I saw his colour. Our baby wasn't blue; our boy was pink!

"Congratulations, it's a boy," the anaesthetist said. I wanted to reach up and kiss her. Everything was fine; everything was going to be just fine.

Trying to catch my breath, I looked up at Niall and cried, "He's pink, Niall, he's pink, do you see?"

Niall smiled weakly back at me and stroked my hand, but he kept looking over his shoulder. I wasn't worried. They would hand us our son soon.

God, I cannot believe he's pink!

Niall's grip on me weakened; his stroking stopped. He was now fully turned towards the baby. I became aware of activity in the corner of the room. I heard numerous voices. I heard them repeat "dropping, dropping, dropping". I could no longer hear the baby. The anaesthetist with the lovely eyes told me they needed to take care of me now and that the baby was receiving immediate attention.

"You knew that sweetheart," she said.

Of course; she had known there was a problem all along. Our baby was to be transferred to Intensive Care Unit 8 at the top of the hospital.

My son, King of the Castle.

Niall looked at me. Our plan was about to kick into action.

"Go," I whispered to him. "Go." Then, remembering, I gripped his arm. "Tell them he has a name; tell them his name, Niall."

He was gone. Niall and Matthew gone. Father and son.

14

Ten Fingers & Ten Toes

I lay in the recovery room and pressed the button every 10 minutes. The wall clock was right in my line of vision. This was good; I could get the timing just right. It hadn't been explained to me why I needed to keep pressing this button but, obviously, it was of paramount importance that I did so. I looked at the other girls in the recovery room; they were all asleep. I wondered why they didn't need to press a button. I reckoned there must be one allocated person per room. I was the chosen one. I had better keep my eye on the clock and keep pressing the button.

The nurse came over to me and asked me how I was. She stood right in front of the clock, however, and this upset me. I didn't want to be rude but I needed her to move. I needed to see the time. She asked me if I was in any pain. I told her I wasn't and, absently, I thought that was remarkable seeing as I had just undergone an operation. I really wanted to ask her to move. I needed to get the timing right. She kept standing where she was, blocking my vantage point.

God, I'm going to have to wing it. I was definitely due to press the button again soon... I'll chance it.

I pressed the button, and she finally moved so I could see the clock again. *I got it right! Good blind call!* I congratulated myself. *Terrific; now I can relax again for another 10 minutes.* Just then Niall came in. He must have known about the button and my 10-minute-interval task because he sat in a really good spot which meant I could keep my eyes on the clock, and keep pressing the button.

I heard him say, "Yvonne, things are really bad, really bad. It is not going well."

I was looking at the clock. *I've about two more minutes to go.*

"They couldn't find a line; they just couldn't find one," he continued. "It took them such a long time to finally get one."

I have only one minute to go.

"Yvonne, he's not going to make Crumlin; that's what they're saying. They don't think he'll make Crumlin."

It's time. I pressed the button. *Good, I can relax again.*

I took my eyes from the clock and turned them towards Niall. I saw him leaning forward; he had his head in his hands. He was crying. My Niall was crying. I had known him 16 years, and I had never seen him cry.

Why is he crying? I don't understand. Why is he crying?

"Niall, everything's changed. The baby's not blue, like they said. Didn't you see how pink he was?" I asked him, vaguely aware of some slurring in my speech. "Everything is going to be fine," I assured him.

What time is it? I need to press the button.

My eyes were back on the clock. I sensed him shift and sit up. I hoped he wouldn't move so I couldn't see.

"Jesus, Yvonne, are you listening to me? They couldn't get a line from him. They couldn't stabilise him for a long time, too long." He sounded angry.

But I need to push the button. I pushed the button. *Phew.*

"Christ, Yvonne!" he shouted. "What in God's name is wrong with you?" he demanded.

He looked at the button in my hand and the vacancy in my face.

"Jesus Christ, you're pumped up with fucking morphine. Stop; stop and listen to me," he entreated.

He took the button out of my hand. His anger had dissipated and, very slowly, as if speaking to a child, he told me, "Yvonne, they're afraid we'll lose him on the journey to Crumlin. They're worried about going ahead. They don't think he'll make it!" He collapsed in a slump, and then whispered, "We're going to lose him Yvonne; we're going to lose him."

We're going to lose him. We're going to lose him. Oh Jesus.

I tried to push myself up in the bed and looked around me. The other girls slept on.

"Where is he? Where is he? I need to see him," I said, the urgency of the situation finally registering with me.

I wish I wasn't so... tired.

"In Unit 8, but you can't; they won't allow you out of here," he explained, his face back in his hands.

"Niall, get me a wheelchair and get me into it. We have to get up to him," I insisted, already shifting myself from the bed. I felt energy coming back to me. Niall remained still.

"Please Niall, we have to get back to him," I said, throwing the blankets off me. The nurse saw the commotion and came over.

"I need to bring her up to intensive care. We need to be with the baby," Niall told her, and I was grateful that he wasn't asking her.

"She needs more time to recover," the nurse answered, calm as you like.

Jesus, was this nurse going to be permanently in my way?

"I am going up to see my baby, now!" I insisted. "Please, just bring me a wheelchair."

She hesitated and glanced at the two girls sleeping beyond me. Then she nodded. She was back just as I was swinging my legs to the edge of the bed. I abandoned the morphine pump and, between Niall and the nurse, I managed to settle into the wheelchair. We were off.

Niall's knowledge of the hospital was impressive. He appeared to know every inch of it. If the circumstances were different, it would have been exhilarating. Niall, at top speed, was pushing me along corridors, through doors, and onto lifts. *Two kids... all grown up.* He stopped short of a set of double doors at the top floor of the hospital.

"We're here," he said.

I was impatient. "So, let's go in," I entreated.

He came around to face me and knelt down so he was at my level.

"He's all wired up Yvonne. He has tubes coming out of his nose and his arms and wires running over his chest... and... you won't be able to hold him."

I was still impatient. "Okay, okay; I'm okay with that. That's okay. Can we go in now?" I pleaded.

He buzzed a switch at the double doors and the doors opened. He wheeled me through, and we arrived in a different land. The top floor of Holles Street Hospital is called Unit 8. The place was drenched in sunshine and there were rows upon rows of incubators. *All the sad cases.* We passed a wall of greeting cards and photographs; toddler faces were beaming out at me. *Plenty of babies are born sick and they all get better.* It was very peaceful, belying the underlying turmoil of all who had to be here. I saw a young mother in a T-shirt and a pair of jeans sitting next to one of the incubators. She was reading a book. Her baby was sleeping. That was her world, her baby's world. That was their normality for now.

We turned a corner and the peace was shattered. I saw two paramedics, a nurse, and two doctors. They had decided to take Matthew to Crumlin after all. It was his only chance. I recognised the straight-talking doctor from earlier. On sight of us, the group fell silent.

I cannot see Matthew. As if they had read my thoughts, they parted. *There he is.*

Niall pushed me through the path of people closer towards the Perspex incubator. There were two holes through which I could put my hands. I was motionless. He was just as Niall had described: covered in wires and tubes, with band-aid plasters holding all the lines in place. I marvelled at him. He was just so perfect. Everything so finely tuned. Even his ears—every last fold was delicately placed and perfectly proportioned, like the intricacy of a rose petal. A spec of fluff was lodged amongst the creases of his neck. He actually had creases in his neck! His face was plump and rosy, and his lips were shiny and red. His hair—he had hair—at the base of his head was wet with sweat and, therefore, darker in colour. However, what confounded me most, and pleased me immeasurably, was his defiance in holding onto the pink hue in his beautiful skin. Perfect.

Then I counted his fingers and toes. He had ten fingers and ten toes: ten of each. Not a single one was missing. All were present and accounted for. Funny, I had never done that before—counted the fingers and toes of my children. I had always thought it a bit indulgent when people confirmed this about their babies, as though they would send them back if there was one missing. Yet, here I was doing just that, and it made me angry. Imagine, the detail of his fingers and toes made me angry.

Why all the toes? Why? We could have easily managed without a toe, or a finger even, but we really could have done with a heart.

I heard the voice of the straight talking doctor: "We need to transfer him now. Matthew is stabilised, but we really need to move him now." The ambulance guys were hovering, anxious to get going. I looked up at Niall, his shiny eyes shinier than ever.

"Can my husband go with him in the ambulance?" I asked the doctor, still looking at Niall.

"I'm afraid not," she replied, she really didn't colour things in.

Still looking at Niall, I said, "You need to go. You should be there when he arrives."

"Will you be alright?" he asked, torn again.

"I'll be fine, Niall, really; you should go," I repeated.

Niall bent down, leaned in, squeezed my hand, and kissed me full on the lips. Then he was gone. I was asked to say goodbye to Matthew.

I haven't yet said "hello".

I put my hands through the holes and began to stroke him. I was not crying, but I could hear my breathing had become ragged. A terrible ache enveloped me. I couldn't shift it. I desperately wanted to hold him. I noticed he had a needle inserted in the back of his hand; I had the same in mine. I turned to those witnessing the scene and asked, "Can we loosen the needle some? It looks so sore on him." By way of illustration, I raised my own hand.

The straight-talker spoke again: "He is in no pain, he cannot feel anything."

He cannot feel anything. My little boy lying under my hands cannot feel anything. I removed the fluff from the crease in his neck. *I suppose he couldn't feel that either, but just in case.* I could sense the growing tension around me, they were impatient now. However, before I took my hands out, before I stopped caressing my son who couldn't feel anything,

I looked up at my little audience. Tears that had not come until now, fell down my face.

"He's lovely, isn't he?" I asked them all. There was nodding and shifting but nobody said anything.

Then the straight-talker talked again; she just couldn't help herself. "Matthew needs to go now," she said, and I was grateful that she used his name.

She eased me away from the incubator, and the paramedics, as if suspended on a tight wire, sprang into action. Suddenly they were off; wheeling my little baby, only a few hours old, out into the noisy, dirty city, out into the world and away from me—far, far away from me. I stared after them. I was redundant.

Then, as if from a great distance, the female doctor spoke again: "We took some time to stabilise Matthew, we found it difficult to get a line, very difficult. Your husband witnessed some things that were very unpleasant and disturbing and, indeed, I am worried about what he saw. He may need to talk to someone about that."

I nodded and nodded. *We will do that. We will do just that, when everything gets back to normal. What's normal about my life anymore?*

She continued, "Matthew was without oxygen for quite some time, Yvonne."

I said nothing.

"If Matthew survives, *if,* there is a real possibility he will be severely brain-damaged."

Tumbling, tumbling, tumbling.

"I'm sorry," she added.

Why are you sorry? My baby's not dead. I stared back at this straightest of talkers. I wasn't crying anymore. *Turn off the world, I'm getting off.* Hope had vanished.

Darkness had rolled in. *A beautiful body with no heart and now it seems no little person either. But hey, we had all ten fingers and toes. Why bother? Why fucking bother?*

I sat in the wheelchair. I felt the sun shine on the snot and dried-in tears on my face, making it feel tight and dry. The doctor's face was still in front of mine, her lips were moving but I couldn't hear her voice. *"Brain-damaged"... "Brain-damaged"... No longer "pink", no longer "blue", but "brain-damaged".* And right there and then, I knew what I wanted. I hated knowing it, and I hated wanting it, but still I knew.

I wanted Matthew to die.

15

Life from both sides

I lay in bed, in a room on my own that overlooked Merrion Square in the middle of Dublin City. Government Buildings were across the park from my hospital room and beside that was the National Art Gallery. Up from there, was the National History Museum. My surroundings were certainly illustrious. Moreover, the farmers had come to town that day—in protest. A unique day that saw Merrion Square converted into a sea of tractors. I heard the honking of horns, a loudspeaker in the distance, and the hum of stalled traffic. Of course, I saw none of it. It was the nurses (who had put me back on morphine) and the orderlies who passed in and out of my room, that gave me the running commentary and provided the updates of the unfolding events below my bedroom window.

Outside my door, there was much activity too. Deliveries were made and visitors arrived to other rooms. I heard children's voices, nurses' instructions, and people arriving with balloons and flowers. I heard cots being pushed slowly in the direction of the nursery and nurses running past my door, rushing towards some small emergency. I occupied my own world. I was as much removed from all that was outside my door, as I was from all that was outside my window.

I heard a gentle knock and a slight push of the door, and then the most familiar faces in the world appeared in the crack—my mum and dad. With tears, smiles, and outstretched arms, they entered my world.

I drifted in and out of my drug induced sleep. Every time I opened my eyes, I saw my parents: my Dad to one side and my mother to the other, her hand covering mine all the time. *Hands on a child that can't feel anything.* They asked no questions, they made no enquiries, and it never occurred to me that we had never called them, never updated them, and never told them what had happened. Later I learned that they had spent the morning wandering around Dublin, aimless, apprehensive, and anxiously waiting for word that never came. In the absence of any news, they had negotiated the tractors holding court in Merrion Square and made their way to the hospital in Holles Street.

Upon their arrival, they witnessed an ambulance at the door with two police outriders waiting by it. They told me this was a sight to behold. The baby was alive. *Did they think the baby wouldn't be?* This was "our ambulance". My mother approached the policemen and asked them if they were transporting baby Joye to Crumlin Children's Hospital (according to my mother there was only one sick baby in the world that day). They said they were, and my parents' hearts soared. Hope again. *Had they lost it?* Not wanting to pre-empt matters inside, they stood with these gentlemen in front of the National Maternity Hospital. They had introduced themselves as baby Joye's grandparents, and I realised that Matthew belonged to more than just Niall and me.

Lying in the bed in that room in Holles Street with my parents on either side, I smiled, hearing their story. A lovely picture had come into my head. There was a moment at the front door of this hospital, an interchange between two outriders and two grandparents, that would never have taken place if Matthew had not come to be. As the day turned to dusk and darkness got the upper hand, I became conscious of a third person in the room. When I opened my eyes, I recognised that person as the paediatrician who had worked on Matthew both in the delivery room and in the special unit at the top of the hospital. He was a man from Thailand, with the softest of faces. I had not spoken to him until now. He was sitting to my left beside my mother, and as I made a conscious effort to rouse myself, the expression on his face demonstrated real concern. I moved myself gently up in the bed in order to sit up, and he jumped to rearrange the pillows.

"Hello, doctor," I slurred.

"Hello, Yvonne," he replied. "I wanted to speak with you."

I nodded. Tiredness was overwhelming me.

"I need to be direct with you and honest. We did our very best with Matthew, our very best. We had great difficulty in the early stages…" He paused before continuing. "I did not want him to travel to Crumlin," he revealed to me. "That is when I asked your husband to go to you. I felt Matthew [*keep saying his name, it sounds so lovely*] would not make the trip, that he would not survive it, and I thought that it would be better that he 'go' here with you and your husband, rather than in an ambulance… But your son held firm [*my beauty*] and we decided to give him a chance at Crumlin."

His only chance.

My mother's hand still covered mine as the doctor paused again to let his words sink in. Then he confirmed, "He made it to Crumlin."

I never doubted he would.

"However, on conferring with my colleagues there… the malformation of the heart has exceeded our worst fears, with all main arteries being severely affected."

My father took hold of my other hand.

"It is inoperable. I am sorry, Yvonne. There is nothing to be done," he said in a very low voice.

Nothing—I felt nothing. Nothing came into my mind. No feeling enveloped me. Then I heard myself speak, but I thought for a moment that it was someone else talking.

"Where is he now?" I whispered.

"He is in intensive care in Crumlin; your husband is with him," the doctor answered.

My husband and my son together—that's nice.

The kind doctor with the soft face had more to say: "It is just one of those things, Yvonne—a quirk of nature, one chance in thousands. It wasn't down to what you ate, drank, or how many times you had sex. [*what?*] It was there from the beginning, right from conception."

As he spoke, I could hear a baby crying in another room. My mother stroked my hair. *I hear a little boy crying.*

The doctor glanced at my parents, turned to me and said, "We are going to bring Matthew back here tomorrow… to be with you," he told me.

That brought me up suddenly. "But is that not too dangerous?" I asked, confused now. "We might lose him on the journey back."

Again, the soft doctor glanced at my parents and then at me. "He is stable now; we can bring him back to you safely so you can be with him," he said.

Okay. Well that's good then. I think I'll sleep a little now. I relaxed my head back in the pillows and closed my eyes. I was so tired. I heard the doctor talking to my parents, and I was vaguely aware of my father standing up to shake his hand.

I must ask this nice doctor about the brain-damaged thing, but I won't do it in front of my parents. I don't want them to know about that.

My parents left when it was late, but I don't know when. Niall called and said some things I had already heard. He wanted to know if I needed him, and I told him I didn't. He could not leave Matthew alone. The nurse came in then and she handed me some tablets.

"What are these?" I asked her sleepily.

"Sleeping tablets. Take them, they will help you sleep," she advised.

I smiled weakly.

"Won't need them," I told her. "I'm very tired already."

"Well, keep them there and take them if you need to," she said.

She went about the room arranging things, checking charts, and arranging more things, and I followed her all the time with half open eyes. When she came back by my bed, I spoke to her. "I feel funny," I mumbled.

She turned and looked at me with a question on her face.

"I feel that I'm not really with it," I tried hard to be articulate, but was finding it difficult. Her face suddenly overflowed with sympathy.

"I know, I can imagine..." she began.

She wasn't getting me, so I interrupted her: "I feel detached, I feel funny... strange." Every word I uttered was a feat.

She looked to be at a loss until she stopped and looked at the drip beside me.

"I could reduce the morphine?" she suggested.

Morphine. What bloody morphine? I woke up some. How can I still be taking morphine when I haven't been pushing any buttons?

"I haven't been taking any," I assured her.

"You have been receiving it intravenously," she explained.

So that's what's wrong with me. I'm fucking spaced.

"I don't want it," I said, annoyed.

"You need it love, you need it for the pain," she counselled.

"I'm not in any pain," I insisted, trying to get the awful dullness out of my voice.

"That's because you're on morphine," she repeated.

I stopped, took a deep breath, and looked at her, my face one big entreaty. "Please, please take away the morphine," I pleaded. I still had enough awareness left to recognise that I needed clarity.

She hesitated; she wasn't to be defeated easily. "You will need to take painkillers."

"I will," I answered, like a child who had been given a second chance.

She took away the morphine, and I was back in control. I didn't take the painkiller she left for me or the sleeping pill, yet I still fell to sleep that night.

I woke at 2 a.m. and when I did, I knew I wasn't going to sleep for the rest of the night. I didn't want to. I wanted to think about what had just happened to us. I needed to think about the day we had just had, and I needed to think clearly. I had spent the day floating above it all, not touching it and not feeling it. Somehow it wasn't part of me, and I wasn't part of it. A parallel me, but not me.

There is a baby somewhere in this city that belongs to me, but who I don't know. Up until about 12 hours ago, we had moved as one, we were one. Now we were two distinct entities, in two separate hospitals, and living two different lives. The body that produced him was lost to him, the heart that nurtured him was his no longer, and the rhythm of our lives together was no longer his soundtrack. He was on his own.

I rang Crumlin Children's Hospital. I asked to be put through to intensive care. A nurse answered and I introduced myself: "This is Yvonne here, Mummy to Matthew Joye." Oh the relief of this. I felt near to him again. Somewhere down the corridor from where my voice echoed through the ward phone, my son slept. I was with him again; we were very nearly joined up again. "I am just calling to check on Matthew," I explained.

"Oh," she said.

"Matthew Joye," I said again, just to be clear.

"Yes, yes, I know," she said, but she still had some uncertainty in her voice.

I was still waiting for an answer, so I repeated the question: "I'm just calling to see if he's okay and to ask how he's doing?"

"He's... he's fine," she revealed after a pause. "Sure, isn't he coming back to you tomorrow?" she asked, asserting herself.

I had nothing to say.

"Are you okay?" she enquired.

"Yes," I whispered and repeated a now familiar lie: "I'm fine."

I put the phone back in its cradle. I sat staring into darkness, and it all became clear. The message that I hadn't heard before, the lump of fact that I had not yet digested, and the conclusion long determined but only now just realised: Matthew was coming back to me, but he was coming back to die.

Light streamed through the bottom of my hospital room door. Shadows of passing feet interrupted the strip of light. Babies were crying and cots were wheeled to and fro, testimonies to the demands of the night shift. It struck me again that everything outside this room was a world removed from me. The crying, the babies, and the mothers—none of it existed in any real way for me. I was closer to another world, a world that existed in another hospital, in another room.

He is coming back to me tomorrow... I need to get ready. He is going to die tomorrow... I need to get ready.

I stayed awake all night, never moving from the spot in which I sat, getting ready for a day I never imagined would ever happen to us. Niall called first thing the next morning and told me that he and Matthew would be back in Holles Street by 10 a.m. —another ambulance and another dash across town. Matthew was quite the maverick at only 18 hours old. Niall asked how we were going to deal with the kids, and if we should bring them in to see him. I hesitated. My gut reaction was no. At 34 years old, I had never lost anyone in my life. They were just children; how could I do that to them?

"He's their baby brother," Niall reminded me gently, his voice slightly breaking.

He was right. Matthew did not belong to just Niall and me.

I cleaned myself and dressed in the cotton-lined, pink, satin pyjamas I had planned for the birth photo. *We will get the photo yet.* I then packed his changing bag with four nappies, Sudocrem, baby powder, and some cotton pads. Everything was new; everything was fresh. I picked two babygros to put in the bag along with two crisp white vests, a white cap, and some mittens for his hands. Everything was done. It was 7.30 a.m. on Saturday, 11 January 2003.

I sat down on the bed. I placed the nappy bag beside me, and I waited for my husband and child to come back to me. The room was dark. There were no flowers here and no cards. There was a certain neatness to my surroundings. I walked over to the window and looked out over Merrion Square. The roads were very quiet. This Saturday in early January, the hangover of Christmas still prevailed. It seemed the world was not quite ready for real life yet. I was not ready for real life yet.

The nurses came and went, taking my temperature and taking my blood pressure. They apologised self-consciously for the noise levels the night before and for the amount of crying babies. I told them I hadn't heard them. The breakfast lady came in, and I recognised her from my previous three stays. She recognised me too. She didn't seek out the non-existent cot in my room but kindly asked after all my children. I told her that if she was around at lunchtime, she'd get to see the whole gang of us. She told me she loved my pink pyjamas and she left the room, pushing and clattering her trolley of trays before her.

The morning dragged on. I turned on the TV, and I turned it off again. I turned on my mobile phone. There were a number of missed calls but no messages. What message would you leave? I wondered about this. At 9.45 a.m. I asked the nurse to bring me up to the intensive care unit. I wanted to be there before Niall and Matthew arrived. It was very clammy in the hospital, and the satin pyjamas were sticking to me. We entered through the double doors to Unit 8. We didn't go fully through, but she brought me to a landing to the right, a place once again drenched in sunshine. It was a room with a view. She parked me there as she continued on into the depths of Unit 8.

I looked out over the familiar landmarks of the city. I thought about all the different lives being lived right there in front of me. I thought of Niall. I wondered whether he had ever stood in this landing as a matter of routine when on business. Had he gazed out this very window? Did he ever anticipate his workplace would become a sanctuary for his fourth child?

How is Niall? I'd asked him that question a thousand times since yesterday, and he had asked me a thousand times back: "How are you?" It was a vacant question, met with a vacant reply. There was no substance at either end. We had not gotten to that yet. We were too busy living the event. To me, Niall seemed in control. He always remembered what the doctors said and could always relate things clearly back to me. Yet, we spent the biggest milestone in our lives apart. Matthew's life with us was not shared by us. Niall's thoughts in the dark hours of the night were unknown to me. *How is Niall?* I didn't know. *How am I?* I didn't know. Physically, my body was a sticky mess, but my hands were stone cold. Mentally, I was scared. I knew only two things about what would happen that day: my kids would visit their baby brother, and their baby brother would die.

"Hello there," a voice spoke from behind me.

I turned around and my big handsome man was walking towards me. He was smiling, and his teeth looked very white. He was wearing a shirt with short sleeves and old faded jeans. His arms looked strong and dark. However, there was an underlying paleness to his face that I had never seen before. His eyes were not shiny anymore, but dark, and he had a slight tick in his cheek as if to suggest that behind the smile he was grinding his teeth. *Is Niall scared too?*

"You look lovely," he told me, and next thing I knew I was blushing.

"Are you okay?" he asked me.

I nodded in response. "You?" I asked.

"Tired."

"Thanks Niall," I told him softly.

"For what?" he asked, coming over, and sitting on the sill with his back to the city, facing me at my level.

"For minding him," I said, looking into those dark pools.

He looked over his shoulder at the view behind him. When he turned back a minute later he said, "He should be here shortly. I left just as they were preparing to leave in the ambulance."

"Why don't they let us travel with him?" I asked, thinking it probably didn't matter much now anyway.

He shrugged. "Policy," he said.

I still hadn't told him about the "brain-damaged" conversation I had had with the straight-talking doctor.

"They were brilliant in Crumlin," he went on. "They really looked after him."

I was instantly jealous. *I would have looked after him.*

Then he showed me a picture. It was a picture of Matthew. He was lying on a child's patterned sheet. The tubes and the tapes were still so very evident, but all I really saw was his face and his head. He had on a blue hand-knit cap.

"The hat?" I enquired.

"The nurses gave it to him so he wouldn't be cold," he explained, and I instantly loved the bones of those strangers who took care of him.

Gazing at the photograph, I longed like nothing before to put my hand on the head of the baby in the picture and feel his heat emanate through that tiny cap. Suddenly, we heard the double doors bang open behind us. Niall stood up from the sill and turned me round in my wheelchair to face Matthews's very own entourage. Through the personnel pushing their precious load, I caught sight of a moving cot, a dash of blue, and some pink skin. *Still pink!*

"That's him Yvonne," Niall said.

I suddenly felt shy. "What do we do now?" I whispered.

"We go in," he answered, already pushing me forward.

"Wait, do I look alright?" I asked him.

"Gorgeous!"

Niall pushed me further into the unit to the spot where they had "parked" Matthew's cot. I noticed the girl, the mother who had been there the day before, was there again, in that peaceful environment. I wanted to be her. This time, everyone left us. It was just Niall and me, alone at last with Matthew. He had nothing on him but a nappy and the blue cap from the picture. He had broad shoulders and a tapered little waist. His limbs, fingers, and toes were long and slim. *He is his father's son.* His little head was turned to the side. He had a wire coming down the side of his neck and another wire pasted with a plaster to his chest. He had a tube channelled up his nose, over which there ran a very large plaster that spilled over onto his cheeks. His mouth was slightly open, and his eyes were closed. *Fast asleep.* The drip was still attached to the back of his hand. *Does it hurt, Matthew?*

My hands hovered over him, not knowing where to start. I brought my fingertips to the parts of his face that weren't covered and ran them over his skin. *Silky and warm.* I got more adventurous, braver, and I lay the full of my palm on his bare chest. An ache that had been with me since the day before suddenly faded away. I ran my two hands down his little legs simultaneously, culminating in capping both soles of his feet in my hands. *Do you remember these Niall?* He was so warm, so fleshy, and so perfect. I leaned in and put my cheek to his face and his chest. Then I ran my face down the length of him. I could not stop feeling him, drinking him in, and loving him. For so long he had been discussed, analysed, expected, negotiated, and dreaded. Now he was here, and to the naked eye he was all that he was meant to be—a warm, pink, healthy baby.

"Can I take him out and hold him; can I do that?" I asked of no one in particular.

The nurse approached us and looked at both Niall and I. "Are you ready?" she asked.

It must have only been me that looked confused for it was to me that she addressed her next sentence: "You can of course hold him, but to do that we would have to disconnect him from the medications he is on… and his lifelines." Then she asked, "Are you ready to let him go?"

Let him go? Let him go? I only just got him back.

"No, don't worry," I told her. "I don't need to hold him. I don't need to do that. This is just fine, just fine the way it is." She nodded and was just about to move away when I asked her, "Can I change his nappy? In his cot, I mean? With everything in place?" *You won't have to disconnect anything.*

She smiled and said, "Of course you can."

All that time, I had his changing bag on my lap. I took out his red and white babygro, his white vest, a clean nappy, the powder, the Sudocrem, and the cotton pads. The nurse brought me over a little glass bowl of water, and I began to top and tail my new baby. I removed the nappy that was already on him. I saw it was stained and my heart soared. His mark on life! I cleaned him as I had done his brothers and sister before him. When I turned to Niall to share the moment, I saw his eyes had become shiny again, and his nose had begun to run.

"I wonder would he be thirsty?" I asked, again of nobody in particular.

The nurse approached us (I suppose she must have been observing us from a distance) and assured us that the medicines were taking care of everything.

The medicines are taking care of everything. Not me. Not Niall. I worked slower now. *The medicines are taking care of everything.* I stopped when I came to his umbilical stump. I couldn't move; I just stared at it. That was what had kept him to me and kept him alive for all this time —his lifeline. But it was now redundant; the medicines were taking care of everything. All that was left for it to do was to wither away and die, in time. We would not see that happen though. I looked again to Niall. Under normal circumstances he found this to be the only squeamish thing about newborn babies, but he couldn't take his eyes off it. I think he might have been thinking the same thing as me.

Everything became a blur through the mist that had formed in my eyes. I fastened the nappy, slipped on his vest, and negotiated the fitting of the babygro on him, all the time taking care of the various wires and tubes attached to his little body. The nurse oversaw this, but Niall had to intervene on more than one occasion because the dexterity of my fingers had abandoned me; my movements were clumsy and inexpert. Before putting the little blue cap back on his head, I buried my face in it and drank in his smell. Niall stepped forward and pulled the blanket about him, tucking him in. He leaned in and kissed his cheek. I thought my heart would smash. Then I heard a movement behind us, and a nurse I recognised from the ward came forward.

"Your children are here," she told us.

What time is it? How long have we been here?

We looked at each other. We had agreed that the kids would see Matthew as a normal baby not wired and covered in tubes as he was. Niall had explained to them that Matthew was not going to live but, in so far as this situation would allow, we were resolute that this be as natural and as positive an experience as possible for them. I had never expected this for any of my children. We thought it best that Matthew be accessible to them and that they see the baby I had carried for so long. We wanted for them to be able hold him and kiss him even.

Now they are here, how can we do this?

Niall saw my indecision but wanted me to be clear.

"If we take all the wires away, you know what it'll mean, don't you?" he asked, looking directly at me.

The medicines are taking care of everything.

I looked to the nurse again. "Is there a priest in the hospital? Can we have him baptised?" The nurse nodded and moved away. I turned back to Niall. "I would like my parents to be his godparents. Can we do that?" I asked him. *The one grandchild they will outlive.*

"I'll get them," he said.

And so it was that my Mum and Dad came to be godparents to my youngest child, and as the priest presented them as such, an enormous wave of guilt swept over me. I looked at them, sombre in their commitment to duties they would never need to fulfil. I couldn't help but feel pain of another kind. My parents, married for 44 years and grateful that much of life's hardships were behind them, were now left standing on the edge of one of life's valleys. It was all my fault. When the christening was over, and the priest was gone, my parents left to rejoin the kids in my hospital room, awaiting our arrival.

The nurse looked at us. "Are you ready?" she asked again.

Are we ready? Never. Could we leave him to exist on a diet of drugs until we are?

The nurse placed him in my arms and began the "disconnection". I started to sing a lullaby. She removed the tapes, the plasters, the tubes, and the needles. It was a lullaby I sing to my other children when they cannot sleep, or when they are hurting, or just when they ask me to sing it. This was an extraordinary moment. As the nurse unravelled the last line and released him completely from all artificial support, the tears that fell from my eyes were joyous because, for those few short moments, the medicines weren't taking care of everything, we were. The "disconnection" had meant our connection. A wonderful prize with a high price—to hold him as our own we had to let him go forever. Still breathing, I handed Matthew to Niall. I wanted Matthew to die in his father's arms. Niall had been with him for all of his short life, I though it right he should be with him as it closed. With one long gasp and one short one, Matthew left us.

As Niall wheeled me one last time from Unit 8 at the top of Holles Street Hospital, our baby in my arms, I noticed the sun had continued to shine and the day had continued to be. Our lives on the other side of Matthew had begun. We had looked at life from both sides now.

16

A place in the mountains

"I'll tell you what I can see," I heard Niall's voice bellow down the phone. He was competing with the mountain winds and they were stealing his voice from me. "I am standing with my back to Three Rock Mountain, to my left in the distance is the golf course, and to my right is the M50." The shouting continued: "The mountains are all around, and it is very much the same view we have from home, even the background noise is the same to home—the drone of the M50—I like that part."

Niall was in Kilmashogue Cemetery in the Dublin Mountains and he was choosing a plot for Matthew.

"Is it nice?" I shouted back, even though I was in the warmth of my hospital bed.

"It is Yvonne; I think you'll really like it."

A smile came through in my voice. "I hope so," I said. "This has to do you and me too, you know."

Niall laughed, and then softly, a lull in the wind kept him audible. "It is not lonely, and it is not scary," he said, more to himself than to me. Then he added, "It's as near to home as we can take him, Yvonne."

Decision made. We had a place in the mountains. I lay back in the hospital bed and, once again, I was alone with my thoughts. They made for good company as there were so many of them. It was Sunday morning, but my mind kept pulling me back to Saturday, a day with so many layers that to contemplate a new day entirely, was a leap too far.

Coming down from Unit 8 the day before, and upon entering my hospital room, we were met with a babble of greetings. The kids had rushed forward, hyperactive from being contained for too long. To an outside innocent observer, we were a happy scene: Mum and Dad, new baby, three very excited older children, a set of grandparents trying to be all things to everyone, and Dermot and Frances, aunt and uncle with cameras in hand, who had been with us at every juncture of this journey. A variety of poses were struck. The children were asked to stand unnaturally still, smiles were pasted to our faces in a forced sense of normality, and the air was filled with shaky laughter.

Then, suddenly, Adam asked, "Why is Matthew black?"

The babble continued, and the ruckus drowned him out so I ignored him, but he persisted. "Why are his lips black?"

I couldn't ignore him again. "Sometimes babies can be quite dark when they are born," I answered in an attempt to retain a sense of normality. "But do you like him? Can you believe it? This is your baby brother, here at last."

"Is he dead?" he asked simply. At seven years of age he had asked the question that no adult in the room wanted to know or indeed answer. Though the children knew Matthew was going to die, I didn't want them to believe that the baby in my arms was dead. I had underestimated my eldest child.

As best I could, trying to avoid the harshness of his question, yet answering him as truthfully as possible, I told him, "He is going away from us as we are speaking Adam; let's make it nice for him." Then I pointed to the window and he followed my direction. The sky was blue and cloudless. "What do you think Adam, a good day for a birthday party? Because you know there will surely be one in heaven today."

Luke was listening in, despite everyone's attempts to distract him and Laura, and he asked, "What'll he have to eat… at the party?" and we conjured up happy scenes of any good birthday party.

Soon, however, the boys were getting restless. The novelty of the new baby waned and they began to misbehave. Laura was also getting clingy. It was time for them to go, for everyone to go. Matthew was getting increasingly colder in my arms, and I was beginning to falter. They all left but as they did, Laura screamed out for me. She wouldn't stop. I was sure I heard her even as she left the hospital and was carried to the car outside. My heart was breaking. One child overheated in a tantrum and another so cold in my arms. *So cold.*

I could not believe all this was happening so quickly. He was changing. The baby I had known, very briefly, was gone. Niall took him off me and laid him in the cot. We were silent. The echoes of Laura's screams were still in my ears, and the picture in my head was of Adam's quizzical examination of his own little brother and the banality of Luke's preoccupation with a party in heaven. I withdrew. There were three of us altogether in that room, but we were each alone and silent.

What is there to say? What is there left to do? I have nothing to do! I am in an angry sea; I am drowning; I am sinking.

I heard a sob. It was not my baby. I turned to Niall; he had his arms outstretched and was seeking my hands. I let mine meet his. He looked at me, and made no further noise, but he was crying. He was trying to ask me something. I leaned closer to him, moved my hand to his face, and I brought my ear to his mouth

"Please," he pleaded. "Please, don't let this hurt our marriage."

I pulled myself out of the water and held on to him.

Niall's parents arrived soon afterwards. They were stunned and numb. We tried to comfort them, but it was hard when there was a dead baby lying in a cot beside us. I was annoyed that Matthew's colour had left him so quickly and that his lips were so dark. I didn't want Niall's parents to believe that he had been born that way. I tried to describe him as he was, but this upset them and my voice faded out. Niall brought them downstairs to catch a taxi, and I was left alone for the first time with the shell of my fourth child. I knew now that it was no longer him. All that I had boasted about was gone. I couldn't grasp how quickly it had happened, how quickly he had changed. *Is this how I am to remember him?*

When Niall returned, I asked him about this, and he told me it was the warmth of the room that had expedited things. Sometimes he is far too in tune with the harshness of life. It was as though the nurse had timed it. She entered and asked if we were ready to have Matthew moved down.

Ready? We have to be ready again? What for now?

"Where are you moving him to?" I asked.

"The mortuary," she replied unthinking, and she and I both winced simultaneously, for two entirely different reasons.

Oh Jesus, I can't do this anymore; I just can't.

Niall moved his mouth to my ear. "Let's remember him at his best," he said.

He was right and I knew it. "What is the mortuary like?" I asked the nurse.

She recovered well. "We will put him in a Moses basket."

I liked this. I had never had one of those before because I thought they contributed to cot deaths. "Is it dark and lonely there?" I asked her. I couldn't let it go.

"No, no, it's actually quite nice, believe it or not. And…." she paused as though unsure whether what she had to say next was the right thing to say or not. She must have decided it was because she said, "He is not alone. There is another baby."

Another baby? What joy! What grief! All at the same time. Another baby lost, but Matthew will not be alone. My relief was closely followed by more grief.

My thoughts were back to Sunday now, as I lay in my hospital room. Niall was on his way down from the mountains. We would bury Matthew on Tuesday. It felt like a lifetime away, but between now and then we would write him a letter. It took us the two days to finish it. Two days that told us how we really were and where to tread softly. *Don't let this hurt our marriage.*

The doctors came and went, sombre and sympathetic and always, without fail, they told us that what had happened with Matthew's heart was just unlucky, a twist of fate, and nothing to do with what I ate, drank, or even how many times I had had sex. *We must look as though we have the mother of all sex lives.* They told us that they would not even run tests on us and that if we were to go for another child, they would be confident that this wouldn't reoccur. *I had my fourth child thank you very much, there will be no replacement.*

Then we came to Monday night. Niall spent Monday night at home. We felt the kids needed some more of us. Also, Fr. Mattie was coming. He was overseeing proceedings, and Niall wanted to go over things with him. He had a lot going on that evening. *A multi-tasker now. I can bury the outfit!* My parents and a host of others had come to visit me in the hospital. Everyone kept talking. I couldn't cope. My stomach started to shift and their faces began to spin. I couldn't cope. I sought out my mother, and she was waiting for me. *I need everyone to go. I cannot cope.* She read my thoughts. Though I was hugely embarrassed, it was a great relief to see her usher everyone out of the room, but not before she stuck her head around the door to tell me she would be back.

I made my way to the bathroom, and by the time I reached it, my mother was already there. My body expunged from all orifices all that was in me. My memory of this moment is not the loss of control of my body functions, nor the sense that my heart was being ripped from me, it was of my mother lying flat stretched out on her stomach stroking my feet as my body let roar at what the next day would bring.

"I cannot put him in the ground, Mam; I cannot put him in the ground. How can anyone put a baby in the ground?"

She said nothing, but kept stroking my feet. I have never loved her more.

17

"Goodnight Sweetheart, see you in the morning."

Niall came for me at 7 a.m. the next morning. I was already dressed, my bag was packed, and I was waiting for him. *But not ready.* It still felt like night time. I could hear the wind outside and could almost feel the rain that was in it. As we left the room, I turned and took one last glance at it. Not to check if I had forgotten anything, but to take in again the backdrop to those memories that will never be erased from my mind.

Silently, we were being led by a nurse. We didn't travel by the main corridors or the wide staircases of this grand old building, but along back passages and narrow stairwells that descended into the bowels of the hospital. From the sun-drenched top floor to the darkness of the mortuary: top and tail. I was running on empty and, once again, I was outside myself, floating. Niall carried my bag and followed protectively from behind. I felt as though I was in a grand castle, being smuggled out. We were at the bottom and we came to a door. It was not the mortuary itself but a room off it. I was cold, so very cold, and I was terrified. I looked to Niall and saw his face was white, but expressionless. I couldn't take his arm because he was carrying all the bags, but I stretched out my fingers to trace the protruding veins on the back of his hand. This was not to comfort him, but to reassure myself, in what sense I do not know.

The door of the room opened and out stepped a female chaplain. She closed the door behind her. I had met her before and she was kind. We had agreed that the short service would take place in the hospital with only her, Niall, and I present. We would put Matthew in the coffin and close it here. The burial would involve our families and our priest, but not our children. *How could they see him go in the ground?*

The chaplain smiled at us, her soft face full of compassion

"Are you ready?" she asked.

That eternal question.

I said nothing and Niall just nodded. She opened the door behind her and we walked past her into the candlelit room. She followed behind us. I was struck by the sight of two white objects: a white Moses basket and a white coffin. A knife ripped through my chest. A loud moan came from somewhere, and it was only when I felt Niall's arms around me that I knew it had come from me. Matthew was lying in the basket, swaddled in blankets. He was immaculately dressed in clothes we had chosen for him. I moved towards him. Once again I found I didn't know where to start. I didn't know how to do what had to be done.

For the past three days, I had tried to contemplate this moment but my mind refused me entry. I could not properly form thoughts, and my imagination failed me. I could not imagine that moment and I had never made any plans for it. I didn't know what I was supposed to do.

My eyes devoured Matthew, but my hands were by my side. A brick against my chest had paralysed me, and I was blinded by my tears which were flowing quickly. Niall held me, and I grabbed him back. Although we were embracing, it was an individualistic act; we were both just trying to survive at the same time. The chaplain then spoke softly over our baby. Her voice was soothing and rhythmic, interrupted only by our alien noises, over which neither one of us had any control. She told us that she was leaving us, leaving us so we could say goodbye. She closed the door gently behind her and our little family was alone.

I moved out of Niall's arms and walked closer to the cot. I stretched out my arms, and I brought him into them. Suddenly I felt calm. I cupped his face in my palm and his coldness no longer disturbed me. I cooed to him, I sang to him, and I paced the room with him. I was smiling. I was okay. I turned to Niall and he was rummaging in the bags. Out of a bag I hadn't noticed before, he produced a series of makeshift toys and cards, the products of our other children's labour. I sat down and listened to Niall explain them all to Matthew. I thought Niall seemed okay too. He pointed out objects of interest to Matthew, including Adam's elaborate drawing of an ambulance, a police car, two motorcycles, a limousine, and a line of security men—the dramatic story of the rush to Crumlin had taken legs. Laura had included a soother. She had had great plans for her baby brother to have one, and she wasn't to be deprived. Luke had included a Bob the Builder miniature. He thought it might remind Matthew of all the banging and hammering he must have heard while inside me. The build had obviously left a great impression on Luke.

We were chatting normally now, and we were smiling. Our tears had stopped. I leaned towards my own bag and I took out the top of the pink pyjamas I had worn on the day he came home to me. I wrapped him in it, with his cheek brushing against the satin sleeve. *I can only give you my smell.* Niall took out our letter and placed it under his arm. We looked at each other and, incredibly, we were okay. Together we laid him in the little white coffin, and we tucked the children's gifts around him. I kissed him full on the lips. We lifted the lid together and just as we saw our fourth child for the very last time, I whispered, "Goodnight, sweetheart, see you in the morning."

We secured our baby in his slumber by screwing in the sequence of nails. "I always thought the whole 'nail in the coffin' thing was just a figure of speech," I remarked to Niall. What a time to learn otherwise. The uncontrollable weeping had left us, however, and with our joint work done, Niall lifted up his son in his white baby coffin. I gathered up the bags and Niall tapped the door to let the chaplain know we were leaving.

We slipped out the backdoor of the national maternity hospital into the backstreets beyond. *The*